THE
Nantucket Way

THE
Nantucket Way

Robert F. Mooney
AND
André R. Sigourney

DOUBLEDAY & COMPANY, INC.
GARDEN CITY, NEW YORK
1980

ISBN: 0-385-14372-9

Library of Congress Catalog Card Number 78-20086

Copyright 1980 by Robert F. Mooney and André R. Sigourney

Published 1980 by Doubleday & Company, Inc., New York

Reprinted 1987 by Robert F. Mooney and André R. Sigourney

Reprinted 1993 by Robert F. Mooney and André R. Sigourney

All Rights Reserved

Printed in the United States of America

Contents

Preface:
An Afternoon at
Gibbs Pond

The idea for this book came to us one spring afternoon near the shore of Gibbs Pond, Nantucket's famous "haunted lake," where we had taken our sons for a swim and picnic.

As the boys splashed about in the muddy waters, we discovered an Indian arrowhead near the beach, and our minds flashed back to the days of the Nantucket Indians, 300 years before. The pond itself was named for John Gibbs, a Nantucket Indian who had been educated at Harvard College, and had returned to Nantucket where he was pursued for a capital crime involving a very esoteric point of Indian law. This first test of the law on Nantucket became our starting point for tracing the development of the Island and its traditions.

Although we viewed Nantucket from different perspectives, since one of us was a native of the Island and the other was a frequent visitor, we shared an appreciation of its history and legends. We agreed this was the ideal place to study the effects of the law on a self-contained community. Nantucket has changed greatly in the twenty years since we started to practice law, yet it still managed to preserve much of its character and individuality. We decided to find the reason why it was so different.

In our travels through Nantucket history, we have tried to picture the people whose lives combined to make the Island so special. Along the way we have met some memorable characters: Peter Folger, Benjamin Franklin's versatile grandfather; Frederick Douglass, the eloquent escaped slave; David Paterson, the heroic savior of lives; and the great Daniel Webster, who learned to appreciate the ability of the Nantucketers. It was these people, and many others, who helped produce a community of highly independent individuals living together in the sea and developing a standard of life which set them apart from the outside world.

As we found the life on the Island was different, we found the law was different, and often brought the Nantucketers into conflict with the political forces of the mainland. Although we are both lawyers, we decided this would not be a law book. It would be a book about an island and the people who lived there, and how they came to establish and maintain a way of life which will not be found anywhere else.

Robert F. Mooney
André R. Sigourney

Acknowledgments

This book was inspired by the late Morris L. Ernst, New York attorney and summer resident of Nantucket. It was aided and abetted by Nantucket's leading historian, Edouard A. Stackpole, who gave generously of his time and advice. It was augmented by the personal memories of several Nantucket citizens and the efforts of our tireless photographer, W. Frederick Lucas. Its research has relied greatly upon the resources of the Nantucket Historical Association's Peter Folger Museum, the Boston Atheneum, and the Nantucket Atheneum. It was carried to completion through the patience and typing of Jean Sigourney and Elizabeth Metcalf. To all these people and the many others who rendered assistance and encouragement, the authors express their gratitude.

Robert F. Mooney
André R. Sigourney

THE
Nantucket Way

I

A Peculiar Practice of Law

Solo law practice is at its best on Nantucket, where there are no law firms and only half a dozen or so practicing lawyers. Nantucket is a large island located thirty miles at sea off the south shore of Cape Cod—a part of, but apart from, Massachusetts. Throughout its colorful history as a colonial outpost, a whaling capital, and a popular summer resort, Nantucket has always asserted its independence, and has adopted a way of life which has often clashed with the mainland forces of American law and politics. This Nantucket way of life is best shown by the Island's experience with the law and lawyers. In keeping with its tradition of self-reliance, the Island got by without any resident lawyer during colonial times and thrived for decades, during the nineteenth century, with only one lawyer in town. Even in the twentieth century, despite the Island's growing population, the Nantucket Bar has remained small.

The Island is a self-contained community that had a year-round population of about 3,600 people (until in the 1970s, when it suddenly leaped to 5,700). Although the summer brings the Island a temporary population of about 25,000, for nine months of the year, the rules of the "Tight Little Island" temper the law in a township where lawyers, clients, judges, and jurors know each other well, often as the result of lifetime associations.

Let us take, for example, one of the most familiar problems of the law: How do you select an impartial jury?

The problem was best summed up a few years ago by the veteran jurist George M. Poland. In his advice to the lawyers assigned to defend some local boys accused of trying to burn down a deserted house, he said, "Here in Nantucket we have the original twelfth-century common-law jury system—a jury consisting of all the neighbors who know the most about the case being tried. You will find these Nantucket jurors know more about the facts, the case, and the defendants than we do, and they know the whole story before the trial even starts. Considering the background of your clients, I would rather take a chance with a judge who might be subject to a little persuasion."

Judge Poland was the embodiment of the law in Nantucket and an institution in its courts for almost half a century. He presided over the Nantucket Probate Court from 1929 to 1952, and continued in active practice until his death at the age of ninety-six. He could dramatize the most minor case and enlighten the dullest hearing with his dry humor and turn of phrase. When one lawyer asked a witness a rambling, hypothetical question, Poland interjected, "That's like asking what would have happened if the hound had not stopped chasing the rabbit!"

The judge was a small man, barely five feet in height and slight of build. He lived simply, lunching on apples and crackers, and carrying his legal files in a green Harvard student bookbag. His native Yankee energy and independence were often exhibited at the helm of his ketch, which he regularly sailed from Boston to Nantucket in his earlier days, often leaving the Nantucket Probate Court awaiting his judicial presence and the Island lawyers studying the weather reports and tide tables instead of law books. In 1931 this journey took the judge five days and while the Island alerted the Coast Guard, his trim craft swept into the harbor where he calmly dropped anchor and rowed up the creeks to his home in West Monomoy. When his wife expressed her relief at seeing him alive, he dismissed the furor as foolishness. "Just stopped to catch some mackerel for supper."

Free from the deadlines, court schedules, and commuting routine of the mainland, the lawyers who practice on the Island usually have the advantage of running their own ship on a flexible schedule. When a summer day turns hot and inviting, it is an easy matter to close the office and head for the beach. Anytime after Labor Day is a good time to enjoy a hunting trip, skiing vacation, or foreign cruise. On the Island, where every court appearance and real estate closing depends on the weather, boat and plane schedules, no court or closing date can be considered definite. The professional courtesy among the attorneys includes handling pending real estate matters and continuing court cases to accommodate their absent brethren. No lawyer has ever been known to lose a fee or a client under this arrangement, and it could not be otherwise, since the next situation may find the roles reversed. And local tradition must be considered over the letter of the law.

One of the traditions and peculiar practices of the Nantucket Bar was the tradition of presenting the presiding justice of the Superior Court with a pair of white gloves—the symbol of purity —whenever the Town and County had no criminal trials to be heard at that court session. In 1959 Judge Frank J. Murray was honored with the white gloves and sought to learn the source of the tradition. The late Miss Grace Brown Gardner, a Nantucket historian, reported that the revival of the Nantucket custom was in the 1890s when District Attorney Hosea M. Knowlton had asked Justice Robert Bishop for the privilege of addressing the court in the interest of reinstituting a custom established in England several centuries before.

In England, white gloves were presented to a judge on the occasion of Maiden Assize, which formerly meant a session at which no prisoner was sentenced to death. In later years, it came to mean a court session at which no prisoners were scheduled for trial. The white gloves symbolized the purity, peace, and tranquillity of the state. When the judge wore white gloves, he did no work. The gloves were usually presented to the Nantucket judge by the sheriff or District Attorney, and they were highly prized by the recipients. They were presented at many sessions of the Nantucket Superior Court from 1890 through the 1930s, and were last presented in 1959—the last year of a peaceful decade. Since then, the Island has had its share of criminal business and the supply of judicial mittens has declined, but Nantucket is still hoping for the return of its great tradition.

When it came to punishing criminals, Nantucket often re-sorted to a standard of justice not found in any law books, and imposed the highly popular and effective sentence of banishment. One of the local District Court judges regularly meted out to the unruly stranger causing public disorder on the Island: "Take the next boat and stay out of Nantucket for two years!" Unconstitu-tional, but effective; the sentence was never declined and never violated. Modern judges have discontinued this practice, perhaps fearful that some judge on Cape Cod might sentence a mischief maker to spend two years on Nantucket. The courts, however, have not hesitated in sentencing young offenders to spend several weeks picking up roadside litter or cleaning the Town Dump for their offenses.

The number of active lawyers on Nantucket has varied from five to ten in recent years; but although the lure of the life is at-tractive, the Island has seldom proved a lawyer's road to riches. For years the three most successful lawyers on the Island clung tenaciously to their salaried jobs as Town Selectman, Town Counsel, and Court Clerk, guarding against that rainy day when private practice might fail to cover the overhead. John J. Gardner, II, the Register of Probate, best illustrated this whenever an off-island lawyer would drop into the Probate Court and mention the possibility of practicing in Nantucket. Gardner would pull out the probate docket book and show him the probate inven-tories of the estates recently filed. Speaking in his deepest and most solemn tones, he would point out to the curious visitor: "Here's one, left $500. . . . Look at this one, $250. . . . The next feller? Why, he died broke!" None of the visitors stayed long enough to learn more about their prospective clientele.

The Town and County of Nantucket is served by all the courts of Massachusetts, and, as it is the smallest county in the state, the Nantucket Bar can examine its judges at close hand. The county's meager courtroom facilities used to lend them-selves to this practice, for the judges of Nantucket often operated under unusually close quarters.

Our first memory of the Nantucket court system centered around the District Court courtroom on the third floor of a build-ing that was built in 1772 at the foot of Main Street. Since that time, the old Pacific Club had served as the countinghouse for

Quaker merchant William Rotch, the home port for three Nantucket ships which contributed their cargo to the Boston Tea Party, a marine insurance agency, a U. S. Customs House, and the law offices for several Nantucket attorneys. (In 1846, the building had become the home of the Pacific Club, whose membership was limited to those Nantucketers who had sailed their whalers around Cape Horn into the Pacific, but still totaled over 100 members.) The old courtroom was located at the top of two steep and creaking staircases, and many an optimistic lawyer and hopeful client climbed those stairs full of anticipation, only to descend soon after with the mournful creaking of timbers reminding them of the Bridge of Sighs which ushered the prisoners of ancient Venice to their doom. The courtroom was sparsely furnished with hard wooden benches for the spectators, two straight wooden chairs for the lawyers, and up front, under an enormous American flag, a remote and sternly inaccessible bench —with a judge to match. The building was never adapted to central heating; if the court officer did not arrive early enough to stoke up the space heater, the winter sessions were often conducted in heavy coats and frosted breath, reminiscent of a Siberian court martial. But in the summer, the slate roof held the heat like an oven and the windows, which admitted every blast in the winter, were suddenly hermetically sealed. There were no conference rooms, rest rooms, or telephones. Consequently, there were no distractions from the business at hand, and court business was conducted as swiftly as possible.

In those days, the Nantucket Bar did not survive from the fruits of litigation. One can hardly blame the lawyers of the day for avoiding the physical and judicial ordeal of a District Court trial; those few who chose to pursue their clients' rights to the bitter end usually wound up with an unhappy result and a disgruntled client.

The old Nantucket Probate Court was held in the office of the Register of Probate on the second floor of the Town Building on Washington Street—another ancient brick building which housed the Registry of Deeds, Town Clerk, Tax Collector, and Police Department on the first floor. True to Island court tradition, the Probate Court was perched atop another set of steep and creaking stairs. The room was just big enough to hold two

desks abreast—one for the judge and one for the register—while
the lawyers clustered around a single counsel table forming a "T"
from the improvised bench, all participants sitting within three
feet of each other. On a busy day the waiting parties, witnesses,
and lawyers spilled out into the hall, down the stairs, and often
into the parked cars outside the building. But despite the
crowded conditions, the old courtroom maintained a sense of tradition and dignity from its hallowed furnishings that had
witnessed decades of litigation. The crowded atmosphere reminded one of the classic accommodations of the British Courts
of Justice. Amid the oak tables and horsehair-cushioned chairs,
the ink pots and blotting paper, the Judge of Probate presided
with dignity and wisdom over his brief monthly sessions. For the
rest of the year this was the domain of the Register of Probate,
who, for fifty years, was John J. Gardner, II.

Gardner used the physical fittings of the courtroom to sup-
plement his own shrewd Yankee ingenuity on more than one
occasion. When a lawyer had a "delicate case" before the court,
such as a divorce involving a local doctor or teacher, Gardner
might advise the lawyer to bring his client over "when the room
was not too crowded," preferably 8:00 A.M. or during the lunch
hour. By the close of all the formalities, when the grateful
parties had departed the premises, Gardner could blandly inform
an inquiring reporter or the local gossip looking for the scandal,
"Why, that case is all over and done with; the judge heard it
right here in open court. Where were you?"

The most outstanding feature of the old Probate courtroom
was the solid wall of books—hundreds of thick, cowhide-bound
volumes of old Federal and Admiralty cases which usually had
nothing to do with probate law, but remained a fixture of the
courtroom for a century. When asked why they had not been
disposed of years ago, Gardner explained, "When I was young
and new to this job, once in a while somebody in Town would
come in and tell me he was thinking of running for my job. I
would tell him that was all right with me, but it was a tough job
to learn, and the first thing you had to do was read all those
books over there." And with a sweep of his arm toward the formidable pile of dusty legal lore, he would sweep another candidate

off the ballot, and so he remained Register of Probate for fifty years.

The modern-day practitioner in Nantucket does not have the benefit of these rustic facilities and the homespun brand of justice they meted out, for in 1965 a modern brick building was erected on Broad Street to house all the Town and county offices, courts, and Registry of Deeds. Here was an opportunity for the Nantucket lawyer to spend his entire professional career under one roof free from the delays and frustrations of traffic jams, trains, and taxicabs. Consequently, the local lawyers swarmed the new court house like bees to the hive, and the block west of the Town Building became the new locale of many Nantucket practices. This move has made Broad Street the "court end" of Town, as Main Street had been in the past and today the Nantucket lawyer thus spends much of the day shuffling in and out of what is called the Town Building. Although the courts are still located on the second floor, these modern stairs do not creak.

Just a stone's throw away from the Nantucket Court House are several popular hostelries and watering places, amenities which many of the imposing and impressive court houses on the mainland are notoriously lacking. Thus visiting justices, attorneys and parties often lodge at the Jared Coffin House at the head of Broad Street, and the establishment's Tap Room is always prepared for the quick lunches and hurried refreshments that are dictated by pressured court schedules. In this manner a great public need is met and public convenience is well served; for if you cannot find a lawyer in his office, you need not look far.

A common complaint about attorneys practicing in a small town like Nantucket centers around the possibility of conflicts of interest. Since an Island lawyer deals with an individual who has his business, social, and family relations intertwined in the Island community, the lawyer is constantly confronted with conflicts that could not be otherwise. The subject was recently faced by District Attorney Philip A. Rollins when called upon to investigate an election dispute in the tiny town of Gay Head on Martha's Vineyard. Each side was accusing the other of having a conflict of interest. "What can you expect," the prosecutor asked, "in a town with one hundred adult inhabitants, a third of whom are named Vanderhoop?"

The Island has wrestled with this problem for years, and back in 1880, the Nantucket Bar—which consisted of one lawyer—portrayed the handling of the dilemma:

> But, if through natural perversity, men who have differences cannot, or will not, settle them, one goes to the Bar and asks him to begin a suit . . . the other party goes to the Bar to defend him. The Bar is embarrassed. To take a retainer from both sides is unprofessional. He is acquainted with, and it may be he is the personal friend of both parties to the issue. He is a lonesome lawyer on a lonely isle. Feelings of common humanity will not permit him to throw the weight of his knowledge and experience and skill in favor of one side when there is no one to advocate the cause of the other. Glad visions of fees are snuffed out in the twinkling of an eye. By natural gravitation he falls into the position of a peacemaker . . . and suggests a basis for settlement, which, though unsatisfactory to one and perhaps both, each feels bound to accept. For the sacrifices he makes, he may get their joint and several thanks; or he may not. He has accepted a retainer from neither, nor has he begun or defended an action. Indeed, by his influence, they have been debarred the luxury of a lawsuit. Hence neither party feels that the Bar is entitled to a fee and he is too modest to ask for one.[1]

The problem often arises in domestic cases. For example, when a divorce is impending both the husband and wife may turn to "their" lawyer, who is now faced with a couple he has known for years and represented in other legal matters. What can he do? On the practical level, before any legal action is started, he may try to reconcile them one way or another. If this is successful, the lawyer may earn some personal satisfaction, but, like his brethren of 1880, no fee. And if this fails, he is ethically re-

[1] "The Nantucket Bar," *Credible Chronicles of the Patchwork Village*, E. T. Underhill, 1886.

quired to decline the pleas of both parties—for the law in its wisdom requires that a lawyer whom both parties want, must send the couple to more partisan champions for their domestic donnybrook.

The Island lawyer does not live high above the sidewalk, safely barricaded behind doormen, receptionists, secretaries, and closed doors. His door must always be open to the public, for the public is his only source of business. He may have to conduct business on the sidewalk, in the post office, or in the client's kitchen, for some clients prefer it that way; the lawyer who insists they call for an appointment may never see them again. The Island lawyer must remember that his clientele is highly independent and dead serious about its law business. The legal affairs often involve personal pride and family honor, which are primary considerations in a small town. As every lawyer knows, there are times when the outcome of a lawsuit will not satisfy either side, but the Nantucketer will always know where to place the blame. The traditional Nantucket attitude toward the legal system is best portrayed by one battered islander, who upon leaving the courtroom after a long and discouraging trial, turned to the bench and fired the parting shot, "I don't understand it, Judge, you made everybody swear to tell the truth—except the lawyers!"

2

The Ransom of John Gibbs

The English claim to North America was based on the fifteenth-century voyages of John Cabot. The voyages of later explorers supported this claim. In 1602 Bartholomew Gosnold sailed west from England and first sighted land in Latitude 42° North which he named Cape Cod. He then cruised past Nantucket and Martha's Vineyard to the island of Cuttyhunk, where he landed briefly before returning home. Cuttyhunk is the last island in a chain of small islands extending out from the bottom of Cape Cod which Gosnold named the Elizabeth Islands in honor of his Queen. Following this short voyage, the English Crown claimed the Cape and Islands which Gosnold had sighted by the right of discovery. Years later, the United States Supreme Court reaffirmed the original principle that discovery gives exclusive title of the land discovered to the sovereign of the discoverer.

The law of discovery made scant provision for the rights of the small aboriginal population thinly scattered throughout North America.

> . . . . [T]he only source of title to the vacant and un-
> settled lands of this portion of the continent, claimed by
> the crown of England by right of discovery, was a grant
> from the King. . . . The theory universally adopted

. . . was that the Indians found upon this continent had no legal title to the soil . . . and . . . no fee in the land, but only a temporary right of occupancy, for which it was perhaps equitable to make them some allowance.[1]

On Nantucket, this fundamental principle of law was applied somewhat differently than it was on the mainland. Here the realities of the situation overwhelmed legal theory. The Nantucket way of dealing with the Indians proved far wiser than the mainland way.

In 1641 Thomas Mayhew and his son bought Nantucket, Martha's Vineyard, and the Elizabeth Islands from Lord Sterling and Sir Ferdinando Gorges. Sterling and Gorges held conflicting royal grants, and the Mayhews obtained deeds to the islands from both of them. The deeds, obtained at the cost of only a few pounds, gave the Mayhews unquestionable legal title to a large, unsettled island empire.

Thomas Mayhew, Sr., was one of the first Puritan settlers of Massachusetts and was an early member of the Massachusetts General Court.[2] He had arrived in Medford in 1631 and had tried to make a go of various business ventures in the Boston area, but the outbreak of civil war in England had cut off imports and had ruined him. Although he was middle-aged, he gambled his remaining capital on starting a new career developing the remote and unsettled islands. Thomas Mayhew, Jr., was a young Puritan minister who became deeply involved in missionary work among the Indians. Consequently, the settlement of the islands began as a business venture on the part of the father and a religious mission on the part of the son.

Settling Nantucket was a formidable undertaking; the Island measures roughly fifty square miles and lies far off the coast. At the time of settlement, there were approximately 1,500 Indians living on the Island. The Mayhews could not recruit enough people to start settlements on all their islands, so they began by establishing one tiny settlement of half a dozen families at what is

---

[1] Opinion of Chief Justice Lemuel Shaw in *Commonwealth* v. *City of Roxbury*, 75 Mass. 451, 478 (1857).

[2] I.e., the legislature. Today, the Massachusetts Legislature, which now consists of a Senate and a House of Representatives, is still formally called "The Great and General Court."

now Edgartown on Martha's Vineyard. The Vineyard is twice the size of Nantucket and had twice the Indian population, but it was much easier to get to from the mainland. Although the Mayhews concentrated most of their energies on the Vineyard, they still made occasional trips to Nantucket in an attempt to convert the Indians.

In 1644 the Mayhews called a conference of all the Indian chiefs of Nantucket, Martha's Vineyard, and the Elizabeth Islands. While the Cross of St. George floated over their Edgartown settlement and the chiefs stood with their bronzed arms folded, Thomas Mayhew, Sr., announced that he was anxious to buy land from them. He told them that he would pay them for every strip of land occupied by the white men. The Indians weren't sure what this offer meant, but they agreed to try it.

Despite the fact that the Mayhews had already paid Lord Sterling and Gorges the full purchase price for the islands, they now volunteered to pay the Indians for the land as well. From the start, religious, equitable, and practical considerations on these islands tempered the English law. On the mainland, some of the Puritan ministers of early New England became convinced that the Indians were the true owners of North America, and they refused to recognize the established law. Two ministers, Roger Williams and John Eliot of Massachusetts, became active Indian sympathizers who published scholarly books about the Indians and their customs.

As early as 1632, the Reverend Roger Williams advised the Pilgrims to ignore their patent from the King and to buy their land directly from the Indians. Williams went so far as to write directly to the King, boldly challenging his ownership of North America. He was soon banished from Massachusetts by the authorities, who feared their charter would be revoked for his treasonable legal opinion. Roger Williams left Massachusetts and founded Rhode Island, just across the bay from Martha's Vineyard and Nantucket.

The Reverend John Eliot continued to work within the framework of the Massachusetts establishment and came to be called the Apostle to the Indians. He taught himself Algonquian with the help of a young Indian prisoner and published a Bible in this language. This was the first Bible of any sort published in

America, a particularly remarkable feat considering that Algonquian was an unwritten language.

Algonquian, or Natick, as it was sometimes called, was the universal language of the Indian tribes living around Massachusetts Bay. Eliot taught it to young Thomas Mayhew, and together they proceeded to convert many of the Algonquian Indians, who then became known as "Praying Indians." These ministers had the full backing of the Massachusetts Bay civil authorities who authorized Indian missions. They also received financial support from England from the Society for the Propagation of the Gospel, which paid Mayhew a small annual salary for his work among the Indians.

For sixteen years the Mayhews were too occupied with the Vineyard to develop Nantucket. They pastured sheep on the western end of the Island, nearest the Vineyard, and scrupulously paid the Nantucket Indians for this privilege. They also maintained a few horses near the boat landing so that the Reverend Mayhew and Peter Folger, the Mayhews' business agent, could ride around the Island to the Indian villages preaching Christianity.

The Reverend Mayhew and Peter Folger were young men of about the same age who got on well together. The Nantucket Indians liked Folger and called him "white chief's old-young man," meaning he was wise for his age. Folger was a school teacher on the Vineyard who also served as lay preacher when there was no settled minister available. Both men were avid scholars who became fluent in Algonquian and were devoted to their mission among the Indians.

At first the Nantucket Indians scoffed at the young missionaries and said they weren't stupid enough to trade thirty-seven gods for one God, but eventually most of them became "Praying Indians." The first Indian whom Peter Folger converted to Christianity was a young man named Assasamoogh, who proved to be the connecting link between the two races. He was not a sachem or a powwaw, i.e. a chief or medicine man, but he was a young man of great character and intelligence. When Folger baptized Assasamoogh he gave him the name John Gibbs; John was Folger's father's name and Gibbs his mother's maiden name.

The Reverend Thomas Mayhew, Jr., was drowned at sea on a voyage to England in 1657, which left his father the sole owner of Nantucket and the other islands. Mayhew was grief-stricken at the loss of his son; throughout the rest of his long life, he never completely recovered from his sorrow.

In 1659 Mayhew heard from his cousin Thomas Macy who lived in Salisbury, Massachusetts, a small coastal town on the New Hampshire border, that he and several of his neighbors wanted to buy Nantucket to start a farming community. Edward Starbuck, one of these prospective purchasers, was an admirer of Roger Williams and believed that the Indians should be compensated for their land. The Salisbury purchasers agreed not only to buy the Island from Mayhew, but also to pay the Indians for every strip of land they occupied. The sale of the Island by Mayhew was completed, and the new owners, together with their families, began to move to Nantucket from Salisbury.

Most of the Nantucket Indians had been converted to Christianity by the time these first white settlers arrived. Peter Folger enlisted the help of the Praying Indians in getting the settlement started. Folger served as Indian interpreter, land surveyor, and keeper of the Indian deeds and other legal records. The very first order of business was to pay the Indians for the land occupied by the settlers and to obtain deeds from them. This was done immediately, and the Nantucket settlement began on a high plane of fair dealing between the races.

The settlers laid out individual house lots on the north shore, where the land was high and there was a good supply of fresh water. As the years went by they continued to buy more and more land on the western end of the Island from the Indians, who continued to live apart from the white settlement in wigwam villages scattered about the Island.

The Indians maintained their own separate churches in their villages. The settlers sent John Gibbs to Harvard to study for the ministry, after which he returned to Nantucket to act as minister to his people. Considering their meager resources, the settlers must have had great faith in John Gibbs to make the sacrifices necessary to provide for his education.

Gibbs was not the only New England Indian to acquire an English name and an English education. Massasoit, the Indian chief who befriended the Pilgrims at Plymouth, had two sons who were sent to England to be educated. The Puritans, fond of classical learning, christened them Philip and Alexander after the kings of ancient Greece. Philip, whose Indian name was Metacomet, succeeded his father as grand sachem of the Wampanoag Confederation, and was called King Philip by the white men. Like John Gibbs, he had been thoroughly indoctrinated in English institutions but, unlike Gibbs, he viewed the new order with alarm.

New England had changed radically in the forty years since Philip's father had first helped the tiny band of Pilgrims at Plymouth. The subsequent waves of immigrating Englishmen encroached on the Indian hunting grounds and unsettled their way of life. On the mainland, the white settlers often treated the Indians badly and failed to compensate them for their land. The Indians were trapped between the settlers and the warlike Mohawks, who inhabited the Hudson Valley, and they had little choice but to submit to the new order.

In 1662 King Philip, who lived at Mount Hope, Rhode Island, began to put together a New England tribal confederacy in a desperate bid to reclaim New England by pushing the English into the sea. At this time there were about 36,000 Indians in New England and about 60,000 white settlers. King Philip found it impossible to unite all the Indians, but, had he succeeded, they still would have been outnumbered almost two to one. The conversion of many Indians by John Eliot made King Philip's work extremely difficult, and a Praying Indian warned the settlers. Undaunted, Philip continued his warlike preparations, which included a trip to Nantucket.

The Pokanaukets, who inhabited the shores of eastern Rhode Island and Buzzard's Bay, held dominion over the Indian chiefs of Nantucket and the Vineyard. It was only a short six-mile canoe trip from their home across Buzzard's Bay to the Elizabeth Islands and the Pokanaukets often traveled back and forth. It was easy for King Philip, at the head of a band of Pokanaukets, to island-hop out to Nantucket from his Rhode Island home by way of the Elizabeth Islands and the Vineyard. In 1665 he arrived at the Island with a large fleet of war canoes and landed at Low Beach on the southeast shore of the Island below the bluff at

Tom Nevers Head. The largest Indian villages were located on this end of Nantucket which is farthest from the mainland. King Philip advanced inland to the Indian village of Oggawam, east of the great pond and swamp near 'Sconset.

Philip summoned the local chief, Attychat, and demanded the surrender of John Gibbs, claiming that Gibbs was guilty of mentioning the name of his dead father, Massasoit. Under Indian law, mentioning the name of a dead Indian was a serious crime for which the penalty was death. It is uncertain whether King Philip was trying to exterminate a renegade Praying Indian preacher or to exact a ransom to finance his rebellion. Whatever his motives, it was quite apparent he meant business, and the local Indians quickly joined Philip's men in beating the bushes for the hapless John Gibbs, who dove for safety into the swamp's thick underbrush.

An Indian runner was dispatched to the white settlement on the north shore of the Island, where he breathlessly related the news of King Philip's arrival to Peter Folger and the other settlers. The drum was beaten to summons the men to arms, and the small band of fighting men was divided into two groups. A few of the older ones stayed behind to guard the women and children, while the larger group, led by Peter Folger who acted as their spokesman and interpreter, set off to meet King Philip. The English settlers were far outnumbered by the Nantucket Indians. They were also outnumbered by King Philip's men, but they armed themselves and started across the Island on horseback.

On the way, they discussed the possible alternatives to armed warfare. One alternative was to declare their neutrality in what appeared to be an entirely Indian controversy. This posed a moral dilemma because John Gibbs was their protégé and most faithful Indian friend. If these devout Christians behaved like Pontius Pilate and allowed him to be delivered to King Philip, they would lose face with the Indians and undo all the missionary work of the past twenty years. Yet, if they engaged in a bloody battle with King Philip, the entire settlement would probably be wiped out.

When the settlers reached the top of a hill overlooking the great pond, known today as Gibbs Pond, they were able to look down upon the Indian village of Oggawam which was set back a short distance east of the pond. They heard the Indians beating the bushes of the swamp for John Gibbs and saw King Philip's war party gathered around Attychat's wigwam. King Philip was seated before the wigwam and appeared to exercise supreme authority over the other Indians. Peter Folger marched up to him and, after courteously saluting the Great Chief in his own language, asked him what he wanted on Nantucket. Philip replied that he wanted the body of John Gibbs—or Assasamoogh, as he referred to him—for the capital crime of mentioning his dead father's name. Using his skill in the Indian language, Peter Folger engaged Philip in a lengthy debate, carefully defending Gibbs without ever mentioning the name of Massasoit, a provocation which might have caused immediate bloodshed. Like a careful lawyer skirting dangerous ground, Folger steered the conversation away from the individual charge to the ultimate question of what Philip would be willing to accept to settle his claim.

King Philip was finally coaxed into translating his demands into money terms but the sum he demanded was far too exorbitant for the settlers to meet. Furthermore, he insisted that it would have to be paid in good English currency rather than wampum, trinkets, or souvenirs. Having foreseen this turn of events, Folger produced a sailcloth bag containing all the gold and silver the settlers had. King Philip took the small bag, which contained eleven pounds, and laughed. The moment of crisis had arrived.

Staking everything on one last, desperate bluff, Peter Folger hurled a final ultimatum at King Philip. If he did not leave the Island immediately, a huge force of settlers and soldiers, supposedly already on the way, would march east and cut him off from his canoes. He and his men would be killed to a man.

King Philip looked about for reassurance and saw the Nantucket chief, Attychat, nodding knowingly and his own men glancing apprehensively toward their landing site at Low Beach. Waving his followers toward the beach and clutching the small bag of ransom money, King Philip hurried away along a small stream running out of the pond, which has been known ever since as Philip's Run.

During the entire confrontation, John Gibbs had been hiding in the dense swamp around the pond. With the departure of King

Philip, Gibbs emerged from the swamp and embraced his saviors. Attychat was so grateful for the ransom of John Gibbs that he asked Peter Folger to lead them all in a prayer of thanks. Not only did the Indians join in the Christian prayer, but they followed it up with an oath of allegiance, administered by Folger, pledging their loyalty to Charles II of England.

The rescue of John Gibbs was a landmark in race relations on the Island and the settlers won the respect of the Indians for their courage and quick-wittedness. It was the culmination of the arduous struggle for the mind and soul of John Gibbs and it was a conquest of a sort, but not one gained by fear or force of arms. As it turned out, the Nantucket Indians fared much better by following the wisdom of Peter Folger than they would have if they had become followers of King Philip.

On the mainland, the white men seized some of King Philip's land in Rhode Island without paying him for it. This was the immediate cause for King Philip's War which broke out in 1675. Because they had been treated decently and had been compensated for their land, the Cape and Island Indians remained loyal to the English. Many of the Nantucket settlers' relatives, who had remained in Salisbury, deserted the mainland and fled to Nantucket for protection. The war was a disaster for New England. Of New England's ninety towns, forty were severely damaged and sixteen were completely destroyed. Six hundred settlers serving in the militia lost their lives.

The Great Swamp Fight, which took place in Rhode Island, was the bloodiest battle ever fought on New England soil—bloodier even than the Battle of Bunker Hill. Two thousand Indians were either shot or burned to death, and the settlers lost eight company commanders. Eventually, King Philip himself was shot by an Indian follower who turned on him. His death brought the war to a close. King Philip's head was severed from his body and exhibited on a pole at Plymouth for twenty years. His wife and small son, along with other Indian prisoners, were sold into slavery in the West Indies. The Reverend John Eliot wrote the authorities at the time: "to sell souls for money seemeth to me dangerous merchandise."

All of this human misery was avoided on Nantucket, where

3

World Without Lawyers

Thomas Mayhew deeded Nantucket to ten purchasers on July 2, 1659. The following October one of the purchasers, Thomas Macy,[1] who was a cousin of Mayhew, was fined by the Massachusetts General Court for sheltering Quakers from a thunderstorm in his home in Salisbury, Massachusetts. The Quakers were strangers to him. They were merely passing through his town on their way east, and they remained under his roof for only half an hour while the storm passed over. Macy, who was not a Quaker himself, felt that the Massachusetts law punishing him for his impulsive act of charity was unreasonable. Consequently, he was one of the first of the ten purchasers to move to Nantucket, where he hoped to be free from the repressive laws of the Massachusetts Bay Colony.

In the fall of 1659, Macy, together with his family and a few other settlers, rowed to Nantucket in a small boat and spent the winter on the western part of the Island. Nobody knows for certain what route they took, but they probably crossed over by way of the Vineyard. This was the first permanent settlement of the Island. The main body of about fifty Salisbury settlers arrived the following summer.

[1] R. H. Macy, the founder of Macy's Department Store in New York, was a descendant of Thomas Macy.

In December 1659 two of the Quakers whom Macy had sheltered in his home were hanged publicly in Boston. With drums loudly beating to drown out any last-minute preaching attempts on their part, they were marched through a large crowd to the place of execution. Between them marched Mary Dyer, a third Quaker, who was also sentenced to be hanged. At this time, any Quakers attempting to enter Massachusetts were jailed upon entry, if they were caught, and were often whipped severely even though they had committed no other illegal acts. If they did not accept banishment and depart immediately, they were hanged. Mary Dyer and her two Quaker companions were sentenced to hang for the crime of refusing to leave Massachusetts.

Her two companions were hanged, but, on the scaffold, Mary Dyer's blindfold was removed, her arms were unbound, and, by prearrangement of the magistrates, her sentence was reduced to banishment. Even then she refused to accept the reprieve unless the law under which she was condemned was repealed. The Bay Colony authorities could not and would not back down. Instead they forcibly placed her on a horse and transported her to the Rhode Island border.

Refusing to be thus deprived of her martyrdom, Mary Dyer returned to Massachusetts in May 1660, openly reaffirming her Quaker beliefs, and was again condemned to be executed. Again, on the gallows, she was offered her life if she would leave Massachusetts peaceably. Again she refused. This time she was hanged. Three centuries later, a bronze statue of Mary Dyer was erected in front of the State House in Boston to commemorate her determination. State Representative Mary Newman, the only Quaker then serving in the Massachusetts legislature, led the dedication exercises.

The Salisbury settlers bought Nantucket from Thomas Mayhew through the following partnership arrangement: The original ten grantees recruited ten additional partners, making a total of twenty partners, each of whom held one share of the Island. Fourteen half-shares were eventually issued to settlers who could not afford a whole share. Thus the Island's ownership consisted of twenty-seven shares. Individual house lots were set off among the settlers but, with the exception of these house lots and a few very special situations, the rest of the Island was held in common ownership. By a written agreement signed at Salisbury before the settlement, the settlers agreed to be governed by a majority vote of the shares. They called themselves The Proprietors Of The Common And Undivided Lands of Nantucket.

Although he continued to live on the Vineyard, Thomas Mayhew reserved one of these twenty-seven shares for himself in the deed to the Salisbury settlers. He always argued that his islands were part of Sir Ferdinando Gorges's Province of Maine, a weak and remote colony, and he occasionally recorded Vineyard deeds and probated Vineyard wills in York, Maine, to buttress his claim. Mayhew's deeds from Lord Sterling indicated that his islands were under the jurisdiction of the powerful Massachusetts Bay Colony. For the first ten years of Nantucket's existence, it really didn't matter who had jurisdiction; the islanders were left completely free to govern themselves by the private partnership agreement without interference from any colonial government. Then, in 1670, Nantucket, Martha's Vineyard and the Elizabeth Islands, which had been made part of the Province of New York by the English Crown, were finally brought under colonial control.

In the seventeenth century, the annexation of Nantucket to the Province of New York made sense. The lack of passable roads made it more practical for travelers and goods to pass between the colonies under sail. Nantucket and the Vineyard lie due east of Manhattan, and the prevailing westerlies make the sail down from New York through the protected sounds of Long Island, Block Island, and Martha's Vineyard an easy passage, without the inconvenience of ever having to change course.[2] When the English captured New Amsterdam from the Dutch in 1664, Nantucket was placed under the command of the new English government located at Fort James on the lower tip of Manhattan.

It was six years before the new English government got around to administering the remote islands. On the Vineyard, Thomas Mayhew did his best to delay the surrender of the islands' independence. Then New York Governor Francis Lovelace, who would be put off no longer, announced that he was

---

[2] Today, the annual New York Yacht Club cruise usually terminates at Nantucket as the logical end of the line. Before the Cape Cod Canal was built, Nantucket was almost as close to New York by water as it was to Boston.

going to form an Island Government and asked the islanders to submit suggestions regarding its form. In a petition presented at New York by Thomas Macy and Tristram Coffin, the Nantucketers made five simple proposals; the most important was that they be governed by the laws of England "so far as we know them," and that they be granted the right to make their own, additional laws "not repugnant to the laws of England." Governor Lovelace "pitcht upon a way" for them to govern themselves by authorizing one General Court for both Nantucket and Martha's Vineyard, as the Nantucketers had requested in their petition. The establishment of an independent legislature for the tiny, offshore settlements was unique in American history.

The Islands' General Court was hardly a representative body. It consisted of only six members, the Chief Magistrate and the two Assistant Magistrates from each island. Unlike a modern legislature, the court had power to decide criminal and civil cases as well as to pass laws. The first Clerk of the General Court was Peter Folger.

There were no lawyers among the sixty-five Pilgrim fathers who founded Plymouth in 1620, there were no practicing lawyers among the thousand or more Puritans who founded the Massachusetts Bay Colony in 1630, and there were no trained lawyers among the tiny band of Nantucket settlers in 1660. Stephen Hussey, the son of Proprietor Christopher Hussey, was the only Nantucketer possessing any law books during the period of settlement. He was not a lawyer, but was what the colonials aptly called a "smatterer in law."

As a result of alleged jury fixing on the part of a lawyer, Massachusetts passed a law in 1641 prohibiting lawyers from charging fees for pleading other men's cases. This law had been repealed by the time Nantucket was settled, but there were still very few lawyers in New England at this time. Throughout the entire colonial period, most of New England's judges were laymen. For the first ten years of Nantucket's existence, Tristram Coffin served as the Island's Chief Magistrate without the aid of any prior legal training.

Tristram Coffin was the wealthiest and most prominent Nantucket settler. He and his family held the largest number of shares in the Proprietorship. Although several of the other Coffin

Proprietors remained on the mainland, Tristram was able to vote their shares by proxy under the terms of the Proprietors' agreement and this gave him the controlling voice in the new settlement. As a result, he was continually reelected Chief Magistrate.

His son, Peter Coffin, although one of the original ten purchasers named in the Island's deed from Mayhew stayed on the mainland and ran a lumber business near Salisbury at Dover, New Hampshire. The scarcity of lumber on Nantucket opened a new market for him, and the Coffin family obtained a lumber exporting monopoly to the Island. Peter Coffin became a prosperous lumber merchant and in time was appointed Chief Justice of the New Hampshire Courts. Like his father, he served as a judge without any legal background.

The first General Court was held at Edgartown on June 18, 1672. Despite their complete lack of legal training, the time had come when the islanders had to frame basic laws. Thirty years earlier the original Massachusetts settlers had apologized when they framed their laws by saying, "If we had able lawyers amongst us, we might have been more exact." The islanders felt similarly inadequate, but they managed to do a thorough job and general laws were passed for both islands. (See Appendix.) Some of these laws are still substantially in effect today. It was at this session that America's first Prohibition law was passed, forbidding the sale of intoxicating liquor to the Indians.

The General Court was established by a charter, issued to the islanders by the Governor, known as the Lovelace Charter. The charter required the islanders to remit to New York annual quitrents consisting of several barrels of marketable codfish. The original Proprietors had purchased Nantucket for farming purposes. For ten years they had run the settlement along the lines of an English manor, with Tristram Coffin at its head. As farmers they knew little about fishing, and they were now forced to invite a Salem fisherman, John Gardner, to settle on the Island and provide the needed fish in return for a half-share in the Proprietorship. John Gardner already had two brothers living on the Island, a seaman and a shoemaker, who were also half-sharemen. In August 1672 he accepted the half-share, moved to Nantucket, and set up a cod fishery.

Gardner combined Yankee ingenuity with executive ability.

He immediately recruited a number of Island Indians to man his fishing vessels and they proved to be excellent fishermen. Gardner had little formal education but was a man of action. He bought vessels, built warehouses, traded up and down Long Island Sound, and soon became a political power on Nantucket.

It wasn't long before Nantucket was torn between the Gardner faction and the Coffin faction. The Coffin group was made up of the older, wealthier Proprietors who wished to preserve the status quo. The Gardner faction generally consisted of younger, poorer half-sharemen who had been recruited to come to the Island and practice a trade in return for their half-shares and who strove for a larger share in the Island's government. Under the Proprietorship agreement, a Proprietor was entitled to two votes, whereas a half-shareman had only one. This was the main cause of resentment by the half-sharemen, but there were others. The half-sharemen also felt it was unfair for the off-island Proprietors, such as Peter Coffin, to vote by proxy without ever setting foot on the Island.

The Half-Sharemen's Revolt lasted approximately a decade. There was no clean-cut division of the islanders, as the families of the antagonists became interrelated through marriage. As the feud progressed, many of the antagonists wavered and a few even changed sides.

In April 1673 John Gardner sailed to New York with the first codfish quitrents, and this gave him a chance to gain the ear of the authorities. Governor Lovelace was so impressed by Gardner that he made him the permanent Captain of the Nantucket militia and granted him special privileges on the Island. Gardner persuaded Lovelace to amend the Charter by inserting a provision which restricted the Nantucket vote to Island residents.

The amendment barred the mainland Coffins' proxy votes. It also barred Thomas Mayhew from voting because he lived on the Vineyard. Mayhew, now almost eighty years old, regarded the islands as his personal property, and he was speechless with rage. He never forgave Gardner for depriving him of his vested rights, and when Gardner visited the Vineyard, the old man gave him a tongue-lashing which Gardner never forgot.

The Proprietors held a council of war, but there wasn't much they could do except try to get Lovelace to reverse himself.

Matthew Mayhew, Thomas's grandson, was dispatched to New York with a petition to that effect in early August of 1673. Off Point Judith, a passing sloop informed him that a Dutch fleet of twenty-three ships had recaptured New York while Governor Lovelace was away on leave.

The Dutch ceded New York back to England within a year and England sent out a new Governor, Edmund Andros. Both Nantucket factions raced to New York to court the new regime. Captain Gardner won this epic race because Tristram Coffin and the other farming Proprietors couldn't compete with his sleek, trading sloop *Expectation,* the fastest vessel then sailing out of Nantucket.

When the two hostile delegations returned from New York after an inconclusive conference with the new Governor, they found that King Philip's War had broken out. Coffin relatives from Salisbury began pouring onto the Island seeking protection. Andros had let the Charter amendment stand and, although this amendment spoke in terms of permanent inhabitants and the mainland Coffins were only on the Island temporarily, they proceeded to vote with Tristram. Thomas Macy, who held both a share and a half-share in the Proprietorship, switched over to the Coffins, and this gave them just enough votes to regain control of the Island. The Coffin faction immediately proceeded to revenge itself on the Gardner faction.

To keep the Indians pulling in the codfish quitrents, Captain Gardner often allowed them a tot of rum, though this was not strictly in accordance with the law the General Court had passed prohibiting the sale of liquor to the Indians. When King Philip's War broke out in 1675, many of the settlers feared that the Island Indians would get drunk and go on the warpath.

Thomas Macy, now a member of the Coffin faction, was serving as Chief Magistrate. Macy loved freedom and knew from past experience that unbridled law meant tyranny. He was an ardent prohibitionist, however, and he was convinced, through personal observation, that liquor was ruinous to the Indians. Aided by his son-in-law, William Worth, he confiscated half a barrel of rum from John Gardner because he suspected Gardner of doling it out to the Indians. Gardner wrote to the New York Governor complaining bitterly that the rum had been taken from him without a legal warrant. Gardner, independent fisherman that he was, repeatedly refused to knuckle under to the Coffin forces or to recognize their authority. When he refused to take his hat off in court, he was found guilty of contempt, sentenced to jail, and released on bail pending his appeal to a higher court in New York.

Peter Folger was a half-shareman who sided with the Gardner faction. During his years on Nantucket, he proved to be as versatile and gifted as his famous grandson, Ben Franklin. Folger was better educated than most of the Island's settlers and, in addition to acting as the Indian interpreter, he was also chosen to survey the Island with his surveying rod and theodolite, draw the Indian deeds, and act as Town Clerk as well as clerk for the General Court. All the threads of Nantucket's early legal and political life ran through his hands. Besides performing these duties, he ground his own eyeglasses, made the frames for them, and ran whatever machinery there was on the Island. He was a public servant, miller, machinist, blacksmith, schoolmaster, author, poet, and preacher, all rolled into one.

Folger was an independent thinker who held some unorthodox beliefs. He had moved from the Vineyard to Rhode Island to enjoy greater religious freedom, but he wasn't there for more than a year before the Nantucket settlers felt the need for his talents and wrote offering him a half-share in the enterprise if he would move permanently to Nantucket to act as their Indian interpreter. Folger, who was as fearless and unyielding as Mary Dyer and who insisted on doing everything his own way, accepted the half-share and moved to Nantucket.

Under the terms of their Charter, the Nantucketers were supposed to nominate and submit the names of two candidates for Chief Magistrate to the Governor of New York, who then made the appointment from the two names submitted. In 1676 the Town, still under control of the Coffin faction, failed to make any nominations and on October 13, 1676, Thomas Macy's term as Chief Magistrate expired. Macy remained in office pending his successor's appointment.

In August 1676, King Philip was killed and the Indian War came to a close. The mainland Coffins began to drift back to their homes around Salisbury. Peter Coffin, who was one of the Assistant Magistrates, remained in office even though he returned to the mainland and visited Nantucket only for brief periods.

In February 1677, the magistrates ordered Peter Folger to turn over the court record book to them for inspection. Folger refused on the grounds that Chief Magistrate Macy was a usurper whose term of office had legally expired and that Assistant Magistrate Peter Coffin was in fact a nonresident, barred by the Charter from voting or holding public office. Instead of complying with the magistrates' order, Folger reportedly hid the record book aboard one of John Gardner's fast fishing vessels for safekeeping.

When Folger refused to produce the record book, he was found guilty of contempt and replaced as Town Clerk by William Worth. Folger was not as rich as Gardner and couldn't raise the excessive bail the magistrates imposed while his case was appealed to the New York courts, so he became the first and most famous prisoner ever lodged in a Nantucket jail.

Peter Folger was then over sixty years old. Macy ordered him locked up in an unheated one-room jail in the middle of February —a severe punishment even in those days. The unused jail was then occupied by a stray pig, which had to be chased out, and the manure and snow swept out, before Folger could be incarcerated. Folger amused himself in jail by writing letters to the New York Governor which were full of humor and sly digs at his adversaries. He indignantly complained to the Governor that he was confined in a place where "never an Englishman was put." Meanwhile his family hastily built a fireplace and chimney on the jail and brought in some crude furniture. The jailer soon became very fond of him and let him go home to his wife[3] at night.

Because Peter Folger and John Gardner had worked closely among the Indians, the Indians took their side in the controversy and supplied the Folger family with fresh fish and game during the long months that Peter was in jail. The Coffin faction complained to New York that the half-sharemen were stirring up the Indians to revolt, but no violence occurred.

[3] Mary Morrill Folger came to the New World as a bondservant. Peter Folger helped pay off her indebtedness over a period of nine years, and then married her. It is said she so widened out in later years that she had to sit in a special chair which she carried with her whenever she went visiting neighbors.

Peter Folger was kept in jail for nine months by the Coffin faction, which couldn't make up their minds how to handle him. He insisted on standing mute, refusing even to discuss the situation with an illegal government, which embarrassed them still further. It was a strange incarceration. On Sundays Folger preached from his jail cell, and half the town turned out to listen to him. At the same time, the other half listened to Thomas Macy and other members of the Coffin faction preach at the Town House across from the jail.

Tristram Coffin's favorite granddaughter, Mary Coffin Starbuck, stuck by Folger and went to the jail regularly to hear him preach. Her husband, Nathaniel Starbuck, the son of Folger's greatest friend, Edward Starbuck, sided with the Coffins and regularly attended the preaching across the street at the Town House. Many other Nantucket families were similarly split down the middle.

Governor Andros didn't know what to make of the strange doings on Nantucket. The tiny settlement was in a ludicrous position. There were only thirty white men on the Island capable of bearing arms and there were five to six hundred able-bodied Indian men. Although the Island Indians had been converted to Christianity and had not joined in King Philip's War, they retained many of their savage instincts and were still capable of taking up the tomahawk. Yet John Gardner, the Captain of the Militia and the custodian of all the military weapons on the Island, was a prisoner at large, and Peter Folger, the custodian of all the Island's records, was locked up in jail.

The Governor wrote to the "Magistrates of the Peculiar and General Court of Nantucket" and told them that the proceedings against Captain John Gardner were "illegal and beyond your authority." Folger's case was remitted to the Governor and Council and eventually dropped. To placate the Coffin faction, Governor Andros reappointed Tristram Coffin to his former position as the Island's Chief Magistrate.

The feud continued to smolder after Tristram Coffin's death in 1681, despite the fact that John Gardner's daughter Mary eventually became engaged to Peter Coffin's son Jethro. Gardner reluctantly agreed to provide a dowry of a house lot if the Coffins would provide the lumber for the house. Law smatterer Stephen

Hussey represented the Coffins in the negotiations. Gardner was represented by the obstinate Peter Folger.

Peter Coffin provided the lumber and the house was raised, but the parties continued to fight over the metes and bounds of the house lot. On the wedding day, the deed to the land still hadn't been delivered, and the Coffins became alarmed. If Jethro should die without heirs, the house, being affixed to the land, would revert to the Gardners. At the last minute, John Gardner signed over the deed and the wedding took place, after which the newlyweds moved into the new house. This house, known as the Jethro Coffin House, is presently the oldest house standing on Nantucket.

In 1698 Nantucket was transferred to the Province of Massachusetts and, under Massachusetts law, the local government was no longer run by the Proprietorship. As the Island became subject to the laws passed by the Massachusetts General Court, the Island General Court was abolished. This ended the colorful period of Nantucket's settlement under the Province of New York.

John Gardner lived on into the eighteenth century and became the judge of the Nantucket Probate Court. He initiated a long Nantucket tradition of retired sea captains serving as Probate judges which lasted up until the present century. These sea captains were accustomed to exercising supreme authority on shipboard, and they ran tight ships in their courtrooms ashore.

The marriage of Jethro Coffin to Mary Gardner ended the Island's feud, but Peter Folger never returned the record book. That is why Book I is missing at the Registry of Deeds. Nantucket's early settlers were fortunate because they were able to enjoy a full decade of legal battles without ever having to pay a lawyer.

4

Indian Justice

Early records allow us to slip into an Indian courtroom and catch a glimpse of an Indian trial in progress. Since the early settlers were greatly outnumbered by the Indians, the early magistrates permitted the Indians to set up their own courts for minor offenses. Problems sometimes arose because the Indians were also allowed a right of appeal from their own courts to the English courts. Although the Indians could appeal to the English courts, they had to face their tribal justices first.

The Indian judges often proved to be wise in the ways of the law. The most noted of these Indian judges was James Skouel, whose Indian name was Korduda. He was appointed a Justice of the Peace and also the administrator of the Indian courts on the Island, acting as defense counsel, prosecutor, and judge, a procedure which greatly decreased the costs of administering justice. He was particularly hard on Indians who drank and neglected their corn fields. He usually meted out a whipping of ten stripes on the back for this offense. It is said he even ordered his own children whipped for "rogue tricks" and other small offenses.

Korduda's administration was successful due to a set of procedural rules he adopted early in the game. Whenever an Indian applied for a complaint against another Indian, Korduda ordered both the complainant and the defendant whipped. This scrupulous effort to provide equal justice under the law for all the King's subjects tended to reduce the number of new court entries and kept court congestion to a minimum. It also demonstrated the perfect impartiality of the judge and became known as Korduda's Law.

Indians who were not satisfied with the justice in their own courts persisted in claiming appeals to the English courts, which had the power to reorder the same punishments a second time. There were some Englishmen observing Korduda's court one day when a belligerent Indian was brought to the bar for the usual "rogue tricks" or misdemeanors. One of these observers was Nathan Coleman, a shrewd man and a good friend of the English magistrate, Squire Bunker. After being found guilty and sentenced to be whipped by Korduda, the unrepentant Indian started to grouse and announced that he wanted to take an appeal to Judge Bunker. Korduda turned to Nathan Coleman and asked him in Algonquian, so the defendant would get the message, "What do you think about this great business?"

Coleman replied in Algonquian, "Maybe you had better order him whipped first and then let him go to Squire Bunker!" Korduda took Coleman's advice, and the defendant took his punishment without any further appeal.

Indian justice was limited mainly to acts of individual revenge, carried out on an eye-for-an-eye and a tooth-for-a-tooth basis. They did have one community criminal procedure on Nantucket, however, which seems to have antedated the white men. This was called Medonhumor and was used to discipline juveniles. It consisted of pulling the offender's head back by the roots of his hair and squirting bayberry juice up his nose.

The Island Indians possessed little personal property and had little respect for it. They had not developed any laws of inheritance before the white men arrived. Because they had always lived communally, they could not understand the crimes of theft and trespass. How, they asked, could everyone be equal under the English law and yet not share property equally? As time went by, the theory of private ownership remained a puzzle to them.

Indian deeds obtained from the Nantucket sachems (chiefs) by the early settlers were known as "sachem rights." The deeds guaranteed that the sachems would not allow any Indian ever afterward to claim the land deeded to the English. Despite the fact that the "sachem rights" were promises by the sachems that they would not permit the land titles to be disturbed, they were not deeds from recognized owners.

Three sachems had authority to transfer "sachem rights" on Nantucket when the white settlers first arrived, but the extent of their authority was questionable. Nickernoose and Wanackmamack signed only deeds to land belonging to some other sachem and not under their direct control, while Autopscot, the greatest sachem of all, refused to sign any deeds because he felt it beneath his dignity. These sachems also refused to permit any other Indian deeds to be signed without their approval.

When the original sachems, who had been present at the time of the settlement, died out around 1700, the Indians began to petition the Massachusetts General Court that they had been wrongfully deprived of their land. The Indians never complained that they had been dispossessed by forged deeds, nor that they had been induced to sign the deeds while they were intoxicated. Their only complaints were that the English system of land conveyance was inexplicable and unfair to them, and that the system by which the English seized their lands to satisfy Indian criminal fines was equally inexplicable and unfair.

As the Indians believed that the land was as free as air or water and the white men were co-occupants rather than exclusive owners, they continued to seek justice from the General Court for a period of approximately fifty years. Then, in 1749, a committee of Nantucket guardians, consisting of Jonathan Coffin, Richard Coffin, and Abishai Folger, was appointed to protect their rights. After an investigation and a hearing, the Indians finally acquiesced to the reality of the white men's exclusive ownership of most of the Island.

Liquor continued to destroy the Indians and to reduce greatly their numbers on the Island throughout the colonial period. Early Indian minister Zacchary Hoite, a good man in other respects, became such a slave to it that he was forced to plead to his congregation, "Do as I say but not as I do." His words of wisdom became a famous Nantucket saying.

The English continued to pass and enforce Prohibition laws but the Indians remained well provisioned. In 1700 Nantucket's Representative to the General Court petitioned to forbid trading between the Nantucket Indians and the Rhode Island Indians, who seem to have been the source of supply. The petition was denied. A few years later, the Proprietors of the small, adjacent island of Tuckernuck complained that their island was being used as the exchange point by the Indians who "get drunk and fight and make great Disorder."

Tuckernuck Island is located off the western tip of Nantucket and lies between Nantucket and Martha's Vineyard. It has always been considered a part of Nantucket and, in early days, it was wholly owned by Tristram Coffin. The Indians named this island Tuckernuck—the Indian word for a loaf of bread—because of its white, round appearance. In the winter they used to paddle over there to hide from their creditors on Nantucket and to pick up a good supply of firewater from their Rhode Island kin.

The Indians first taught the early settlers how to catch whales and they proved to have great ability and aptitude for whaling. With the help of the white men's more advanced tools, the industry was soon greatly expanded and the Indians continued to work side by side with the white men at this exciting occupation until both they and the industry became extinct. Here was one area of the white men's world at least which they thoroughly understood and one which allowed them some continuity with their former way of life.

In 1763, a little over a hundred years after the arrival of the white men, there were still 358 Indians living on Nantucket despite the ravages of liquor and disease. By this time the Indian population appeared to have stabilized somewhat to the waves of European immigration. The Nantucket Indians might have gradually started to increase in numbers, as American Indians have done elsewhere, had it not been for one of those unforeseen incidents which abruptly changes the course of human history.

In August 1763 an Irish brig, loaded with passengers, ran aground on the north side of the Island near Long Hills. Fever was running through the ship when she stranded, and two women who had died of the sickness were thrown overboard. Their bodies were washed ashore and found in the surf. Following this, some of the crew landed and had their clothes washed at the home of an Indian woman who came down with the fever and died a few days later. More Indians caught the fever, turned

The Coffin Reunion of 1881. Over 550 Coffins: They started with only two!
(*Nantucket Historical Association*)

The Custom House, home of the Pacific Club and Nantucket District Court.
(*Nantucket Historical Association*)

The Nantucket Jail, 1805, site of the last escape from Nantucket Island. (*Nantucket Historical Association*)

The Nantucket Jail and House of Correction as they appeared in the old days. (*Nantucket Historical Association*)

Pacific Club, Nantucket, 1772, home of the Nantucket District Court until 1965. (*Nantucket Historical Association*)

Justice Aiken and Sheriff Josiah Barrett ready to hold Superior Court in 1907. (*Nantucket Historical Association*)

Abram Quary, the last of the Nantucket Indians. (*Nantucket Atheneum*)

Hon. George M. Poland, distinguished lawyer and Judge of Probate. (*Nantucket Atheneum; photo by Louis Davidson*)

John J. Gardner II, Register of Probate for fifty years. (*Nantucket Atheneum; photo by Louis Davidson*)

Morris L. Ernst, New York attorney and summer resident of Nantucket.
(*Nantucket Historical Association; photo by Louis Davidson*)

Rumrunner wrecked off Tuckernuck Island, a victim of the Nantucket Prohibition era. (*Nantucket Historical Association*)

yellow, and died within a few days. This fever was generally reported to be yellow fever, although little was known about yellow fever at the time. Whatever it was, it was a deadly, infectious disease that spread rapidly through the Indian villages.

Curiously, however, the white men who cared for the infected Indians soon found they were immune to the disease. With the exception of a Mrs. Quinn, who was of Irish extraction, no white Nantucketer contracted the disease, and even Mrs. Quinn recovered from it.

The local Nantucket doctor, Dr. Tupper, likened the disease to the European plague and refused to go near the Indian villages. Meanwhile, whole Indian families died together in their wigwams, which were then burned with all their contents—perhaps at the suggestion of Dr. Tupper—but the disease continued to spread.

When it suddenly ended, exactly six months from the day it had first started, there were only 136 Indians left. Those who survived were either living in the white settlement as house servants, or in isolated parts of the Island, or were absent from the Island on sea voyages. Negroes on Nantucket were completely immune from the disease and people of mixed Indian-European or Indian-Negro blood eventually recovered.

In an age which declared that "all men are created equal," this experience on Nantucket illustrated that—biologically, at least—all men were created differently. This genetic diversity had protected man from extinction at the hands of some single, sinister disaster, but, at the same time, it had proved to be a perplexing fact of life. Laws far more flexible and complex than Korduda's Law were needed to guarantee this diverse humanity the equal protection of the laws.

In 1704 the first Indian was hanged on Nantucket for murdering another Indian. Two more Indians were hanged in 1736, one in 1745, one in 1750, and in 1769 five Indians were hanged for separate offenses, which brought these gruesome executions to a close. English law in the eighteenth century exacted the death penalty for many minor offenses, but these ten Indians on Nantucket were all hanged for murder and no other known executions have ever taken place on the Island.

Indian law punished murderers with death carried out by the victim's relatives, but the English did not dare to ignore these blood feuds on the Island because they threatened the entire community with the dreaded prospect of Indian warfare. Therefore, whenever an Indian killing took place, the English magistrates took charge at the outset. The defendant was given a fair and speedy trial; but if he was found guilty, there could only be one sentence: hanging. Sometimes the Indians murdered white men. The last, and probably the most famous, hanging on Nantucket resulted from such a case.

The story of Nantucket's last convicted murderer, a man whose crime inspired such dread and disgrace that his descendants forsook his very name, is a story that does not appear in the Town's official court records. This is partly due to the Island's revulsion at the murder of a white man by an Indian, and partly due to the bloody aftermath and speedy retribution which followed. The murderer was tried on the Island, but he was tried by a special Royal Court of Massachusetts with Governor Thomas Hutchinson presiding.

Nathan Quibby was a Nantucket Indian who had shipped out as a whaler aboard the local ship *Leviathan* on a voyage which turned out to be both unsuccessful and unhappy. Quibby was a sullen, quarrelsome character among the forecastle hands. He never learned to accept the strict discipline of the whaler. The lengthy voyage apparently made him homesick, and he longed to return to Nantucket and his woman, Judith Quary, who kept his home near Shimmo and who had borne him a son.

The tension he caused in the forecastle increased when the ship returned to Nantucket and, because there were no berths available along the docks, was forced to anchor out in the harbor overnight. That evening a fight broke out among the Indian members of the crew and, as usual, Quibby was the foremost troublemaker. A young white sailor, Henry Gardner, seized Quibby to pull him off another Indian in order to break up the fight.

Suddenly Quibby wheeled about and drove his sheath knife deep into the chest of Gardner, who dropped to the deck fatally wounded. Quibby then leaped for the ladder to reach the main deck, hoping to jump overboard and swim ashore to freedom. Just as he did so, another sailor hurled a whaler's lance at him. It caught his leg and pinned him to the bulkhead until the captain arrived.

Quibby, along with the body of young Henry Gardner, was brought ashore the following morning in a whaleboat. The crowd which had gathered at the wharf to greet the returning whalers was shocked at the news of the killing. The death of young Gardner at the hands of an Indian right in Nantucket Harbor provoked the crowd into a frenzy. Only the calm authority of the ship's captain prevented a lynching. Quibby was turned over to the sheriff and brought before the local magistrates.

Quibby was ordered locked up to await trial by the High Court of Massachusetts which soon assembled on Nantucket. In deference to the delicate racial problem the trial presented, a jury of six whites and six Indians was impaneled. Throughout the trial, Quibby sat silently, showing no emotion even when the jury solemnly pronounced him guilty. Governor Hutchinson, acting as the presiding justice, immediately sentenced him to death. The silent Indian was led away to await his punishment.

Although Quibby had shown no emotion during his confinement and trial, his blood was boiling when an opportunity opened up for him to hurl one final blow in the face of society and its authorities. During his last night, Quibby was held in the same building with another Indian, confined for some trivial offense. A quarrel developed between them and the next morning this hapless Indian was found dead in Quibby's chamber, choked to death by a man on his way to the gallows.

Nathan Quibby was marched to the gallows, about a mile south of the Town, where hundreds of curious and concerned Nantucketers gathered to witness the execution of this violent and unrepentant man. He was quickly dispatched to his doom, with few friends or sympathizers in attendance. His body was claimed by Judith Quary, probably his only friend on the Island, who buried him in his native soil near their home. Tradition has it that their one and only child, Abram, grew up in Nantucket, where his father's name was so infamous that he was forced to adopt his mother's name of Quary. The Town gallows never claimed another victim. It remained standing for some years near the First Milestone until it disappeared in the winter of 1778 due to the scarcity of fuel caused by the British blockade.[1]

Abram Quary, who was reputed to be the son of Nathan Quibby, although the circumstances of his birth have never been thoroughly established, lived out his days as a sad and lonely figure on his small farm in Shimmo, near the spot now known as Abram's Point. It is said that he was a quiet and peaceful man who lived humbly and got along with everybody. His quiet life was interrupted one day when a band of souvenir hunters appeared on his land and began digging near the graves of Indians buried there. Quary took his shotgun down from the wall of his cottage and fired a few shots over the heads of the trespassers. They quickly returned to Town and roused the sheriff who arrested Quary and brought him into court.

In the Nantucket Court, the judge asked him, "Abram, would you really have shot those men if they hadn't moved on?"

"Would I?" said Abram. "I would shoot them and any other man disturbing the graves of my ancestors!"

The judge immediately found himself sympathetic with the solitary, proud Indian, the last of a vanished race. After a mild reprimand, he dismissed the case.

In 1854 Abram Quary, then in his eighties, died. He had been the last male Indian on Nantucket. When the Indians had fallen prey to the yellow fever, the bluefish, which had been plentiful in Nantucket waters, disappeared.

Just before he died, Abram Quary spun the final Nantucket Indian yarn. "When the last redman is laid low," he had predicted, "the bluefish will return."

Sure enough, after an absence of ninety years, the bluefish returned the summer following Abram Quary's death.

[1] The home of author Robert F. Mooney now stands on the site of the old Town gallows where Nathan Quibby was executed.

5
A Coffin Too Often

"Why," off-islanders often ask, "is it so hard to clear land titles on Nantucket?" Large families, migrations, and the peculiar Nantucket way of tying up most of the Island in common ownership for sheep-raising purposes have all contributed to the land's complex situation. The story is best told by tracing the fortunes of Nantucket's leading family, the Coffins.

The family's founding father, Tristram Coffin, together with his wife and five small children, migrated from England to Massachusetts in 1642. He also brought with him his widowed mother and two unmarried sisters. The family entourage which disembarked at the mouth of the Merrimack River from the small, leaky ship *Hector* thus consisted of ten members, none of whom ever returned to England.

Tristram came from the landed gentry and he left England to avoid the civil war. He was thirty-seven years old and had managed to bring some money with him, so he started life in the New World as a trader up and down the river. Besides buying land from the Indians, he also operated a ferry at the river's mouth that ran from Newbury to Salisbury on the opposite bank via Carr's Island. His wife, Dionis, sold beer and wine in the ferry tavern at the Newbury end.

In 1653 Dionis was indicted for breaking the law which directed: "Every person licensed to keep an ordinary, shall always be provided with good wholesome beer of four bushels of malt to the hogshead, which he shall not sell above two pence the ale quart. . . ." Dionis had charged three pence a quart. At her trial, her witnesses testified that she had used *six* bushels of malt to the hogshead, and she was acquitted. Although the outcome of the case had greatly enhanced her reputation for serving good, wholesome beer, the Coffins moved across the river to Salisbury the following year.

By this time, several of the Coffin children were full grown. Tristram Coffin, Jr., was a successful hatter. He married a widow who owned a large house in Newbury which became the headquarters of the Coffin family for generations. The house is still standing and is under the care of a historical society. Peter Coffin, who operated sawmills in New Hampshire, became the family's wealthiest member. The success of his children gave Tristram Coffin, Sr., an opportunity to expand his own activities.

In 1659 Tristram learned from his Salisbury neighbor, Thomas Macy, that Nantucket was for sale. After a tour of the Island, he offered to form a partnership consisting of his family and neighbors for the purpose of buying it. Thomas Mayhew's asking price was thirty pounds plus a share in the partnership for himself and two beaver hats; "one for me and one for my wife." Tristram Coffin, Jr., contributed the beaver hats, and the purchase was completed. The settlement of the Island commenced as a privately owned community with Tristram Coffin, Sr., his sons, and his sons-in-law owning most of the shares in the partnership.

On Nantucket, where he was often referred to as Father Coffin, Tristram presided over his large family like a patriarch of old. The family continued to expand. On his death in 1681 at the age of seventy-six, he left seven living children, sixty living grandchildren, and many more living great-grandchildren. By 1722 his descendants numbered 1,138, of whom 871 remained alive. By 1728 another 444 descendants, had been born and the number of living descendants had increased to 1,128. Nantucket Coffin families remained large throughout the colonial period, averaging ten or more children. About the middle of the eighteenth century, Benjamin Coffin produced a total of nineteen children in the course of two marriages.

The other original settlers, such as Macy, Starbuck, and Folger, were not far behind Tristram in producing heirs who soon intermarried with one another. What had begun as a small community of thirty or so families, became by the eighteenth century one huge, ever-increasing tribe. When an off-islander remarked to her hostess that she had been introduced to a cousin of hers the day before, the Nantucket hostess replied, "That is entirely likely, as I have five thousand of them here on the Island." This was the Island's population at the time.

Despite the increasing population, the Proprietors never increased the original shares in the land. The Proprietorship still consisted of twenty-seven shares when the last of its holdings were bought out by the Town in 1957. With the exception of the house lots and a few other parcels, the remainder of the Island was held in common ownership for pasturing sheep. Over the centuries, the twenty-seven shares became infinitesimally fractionalized by inheritance; this created an awkward situation.

This odd arrangement did not occur elsewhere. Land proprietorships were popular among the early Massachusetts settlers, but by the beginning of the eighteenth century they had begun to wane as townships were laid out and the land was divided into individual ownership. This occurred on Martha's Vineyard, where lumber was more plentiful for development and common sheep-raising never took hold. By the beginning of the nineteenth century, very few proprietorships remained in operation. By the beginning of the twentieth century, the Nantucket Proprietorship was the only one left. Nowhere else in Massachusetts has four-fifths of a county—or forty square miles—been held in common ownership for such a long period of time.

As the eighteenth century wore on, the descendants of the original Proprietors became heirs to the miles of rolling moors and common sheep pastures. It was a rare Nantucketer who did not have one or more fractional interests in the common lands. Subsequent migrations from the Island further complicated the picture. Many of these numerous heirs left Nantucket abruptly, never to return. The chief causes for the large-scale migrations from Nantucket were the rise and fall of Quakerism and the whaling industry.

"Quaker" is the commonly used name for a member of the Society of Friends, a religious sect started in England by George Fox in 1650. Fox had admonished an English judge in open court "to quake at the name of the Lord." The judge good-humoredly referred to him as a Quaker, and the name stuck. Tristram Coffin's daughter, Mary Coffin Starbuck, was converted by Quakers from Providence, Rhode Island. She was known by Nantucketers as The Great Mary, and she soon converted practically everyone on the Island. Nantucket's first Quaker Meeting was held at her home in 1702.

For the next hundred years the Quakers dominated the Island through the Quaker Meeting, which adopted strict rules for dress and behavior. The Quakers are best remembered for their simplicity, demonstrated in their architecture, dress, and lifestyle. They carried these principles to the point of prohibiting gravestones which makes them difficult to trace. Some 15,000 Quakers lie buried in unmarked graves in the Nantucket Quaker Graveyard. These sober, industrious followers of the "inner light" built up the Island's whaling industry and became intertwined with its destiny. Most Nantucketers were Quakers until schisms developed and the faith died out there in the mid-nineteenth century.

When wars threatened, these ardent Quaker pacifists migrated from Nantucket in large numbers to avoid fighting. The first migration resulted from the French and Indian War, during which Nantucket seamen were impressed in the Royal Navy and Nantucket ships were seized by French privateers. In order to escape further confrontations at sea, a group of Nantucket Quakers migrated to Cape Sable, Nova Scotia, in 1761. When the Revolution broke out, many Nantucket Quakers sailed up the Hudson River and settled at Saratoga to avoid the war; an ironic move, as Saratoga later proved to be the war's most decisive battleground.

During the Revolution, Nantucket was blockaded. The islanders almost starved to death, and the population was greatly diminished. After the Revolution, prosperity gradually returned to the Island, spearheaded by the whaling industry, as some of the dispersed islanders found their way home. The Quaker seafaring population remained mobile, however, and they started a whaling enterprise in France, using Dunkirk as their new home port. The British also lured a number of Nantucket whalers to Nova Scotia and to Milford Haven in the west of England, thus continually draining the Island of its population. An undeclared war at sea with France, followed by the War of 1812, during which the Island was again blockaded and the islanders again almost starved, caused further Quaker migrations.

In addition to the Quaker migrations brought on by the wars, the nature of the whaling industry tended to scatter the Island's population. Nantucket whaling had its beginnings in Indian canoes which operated within sight of the Island. The early whalers returned home every night. The larger whales roamed worldwide, however, and as the industry grew, the whale-chasing landowners of Nantucket followed them. By the end of the eighteenth century, the big money was being made off the Brazil Banks, and in the nineteenth century, larger Nantucket ships began chasing larger whales in the Pacific and netting larger profits. These voyages were lengthy. One whaling captain, about to set sail on a short voyage, didn't bother to kiss his wife goodbye because he figured the trip would last only "a couple of years."

Tristram Coffin and his partners settled on Nantucket to farm and raise livestock, not to fish or hunt whales. The unforeseen success of the offshore whaling industry, however, changed all that and, when the islanders pursued the whales into the Pacific and elsewhere, many of them became permanently dispersed around the globe. As the following account of Captain Seth Coffin demonstrates, these far-flung voyages were also perilous. Many Nantucketers were lost at sea and never returned home.

In 1800 in the ship *Minerva* off Brazil Banks in the capture of a large sperm whale Capt. Coffin's leg was crushed and no one on board had knowledge of surgery sufficient to perform amputation except himself and he had only witnessed one such case under similar circumstances. So he called for an instrument used in cutting whale's blubber and then called his mate, and, bracing himself up on a couch, addressed the mate in this wise. "My leg has got to come off or I shall die. I know how it should be done and will show you how to do it. If you flinch one whit I'll send this instrument through you. I am ready. Begin!" And the mate did begin, the captain instructing him how to take up each artery and his leg was saved. When the last bandage was properly adjusted both men fainted.[1]

As the nineteenth century progressed, Tristram's heirs continued to proliferate. In 1826 it was reported that he then had 12,000 descendants living in every state in the nation and in every part of the British Empire. Many of these descendants, whether they knew it or not, still held fractional shares in Nantucket's undivided sheep commons by inheritance. The proliferation of the heirs of the other original Proprietors was almost as great. Occasionally, some of these off-island heirs appeared on Nantucket.

The most famous of these was Admiral Sir Isaac Coffin, Baronet. Sir Isaac sprang from the mainland, loyalist Coffins who sailed away to Nova Scotia with Lord Howe when the British evacuated Boston. He had enjoyed a successful career in the Royal Navy, finally rising from Vice Admiral to Admiral, and had become a personal friend of William IV, "The Sailor King," along the way. He had been forced to part from his wife when she insisted on getting up in the middle of the night and writing sermons.

The Admiral remained very fond of his Nantucket Coffin cousins and he made every effort to free them from English prisons during the War of 1812. One day, as he was touring the famous naval prison at Dartmoor, a jet-black American sailor called after him, "Don't forget me, Admiral. I'm a Coffin too!"

"Really?" inquired the Admiral. "A Coffin from Nantucket? And how old might you be?"

"Thirty years old, sir," came the eager response.

"Well, then," said the Admiral with a firm shake of his head, "you can't be a Coffin because they never turn black until they're forty."

After the war, Sir Isaac visited Nantucket and became so enthusiastic about his Coffin kin that he endowed a school on the Island to educate Coffin children. This was not as eccentric a gift

[1] Allen Coffin, *The Life of Tristram Coffyn* (1881), p. 61.

as it sounds because, despite the various migrations, there were still six hundred Coffin children left on the Island at that time. The school was a success, but the Baronet's generosity cost him an earldom because the English disapproved of a school to educate Yankee mariners.

The devastating wars, ensuing migrations, and growth of the whaling industry, while unsettling the Island's inhabitants, left her common and undivided lands unchanged. The open moors continued to be occupied by sheep and were used only occasionally for picnics and berry picking. The islanders, with their low, shingled houses, rope walks, and piles of whale-oil barrels, continued to huddle tightly together by the harborside, looking outward to the sea. As the original settlers had envisioned, most of the Island remained common sheep pastures, which saved the expense of fencing and provided the sheep with a vast expanse of land over which to roam and an ample access to food and water.

Sheep farming reached its zenith during the first half of the nineteenth century, when the Island's sheep herd grew to 20,000 head and wool-market quotations were given out daily at afternoon tea. In 1665 the Proprietors had ordered each owner to adopt a mark to be cut in the sheeps' ears and had established a severe penalty if these marks were altered. The order remained in effect. The designs were few and simple, but by changing the slotting on one or both ears, an endless combination of marks could be created.

The sheep-shearing festival, which took place annually from 1676 to 1845 on one of the longest days in the year, was the most colorful part of the sheep-raising enterprise. All the sheep were driven into central pens, washed, and identified by the owners' marks. Shearing Day was a social occasion for which all the islanders turned out. It was also a time for romance, and it was at one of these festivals that Ben Franklin's off-island father met and fell in love with Peter Folger's daughter.

By the nineteenth century, the ownership of the sheep commons had fallen into a hopeless legal mess. Wealthy shipowners like Zenas Coffin were too busy making money at sea to pay much attention to their scattered holdings in the commons. Few people were interested in reading the Proprietors' dull records, and fewer people still could understand them. Such a state of affairs was bound to lead to endless lawsuits.

The common undivided lands did not consist of one large, open pasture. Instead, there were many common pastures laid out all over the Island. Each common pasture was called a Division, and each original share was assigned a 1/27th interest in that Division. Assuming that a Proprietor died leaving ten children, each child would inherit a 1/270th interest in each common pasture on the Island; after a generation or two, this resulted in fractions with enormous denominators. The Proprietors hit on a plan for dealing with the increasing subdivisions. Around 1717, when the Proprietorship was completely separated from the Town government by statute, they began dividing the common lands into "sheep commons" instead of fractions.

As there were 19,440 common acres on the Island, and one acre was supposed to support one animal, a sheep common represented 1/19,440 of a share. Thus, each of the original 27 shares contained 720 sheep commons. The owner of the largest number of sheep commons in one of the 27 shares was placed at the head of the share so at least there was one known owner responsible for each share, although it was by no means certain who his co-owners were. The use of the sheep commons became fractionalized as the land rights continued to be subdivided further.

The further subdivision of a single sheep common into fractions should never have been permitted, but every Nantucketer insisted on a share in the common land no matter how small. A man like Seth Coffin liked to feel he had something to come back to if he met with misfortune at sea. Even if he had only one leg left to step upon the land, it still felt good to step upon something solid which he owned and which would not sink under him like a stove-in whaleboat.

One of the purposes of awarding sheep commons among the Proprietors was to avoid overstocking. Some Proprietors understocked, or didn't stock at all, but others tried to crowd more sheep onto the pastures than they were entitled to have. Sheep owners without any rights in the land tried to sneak their sheep onto the commons.

If an owner preferred to stock horses or cows, he could; his shares became known as horse commons or cow commons. Naturally, the larger beasts required more pasturage, and the Proprietors decreed that one hundred sheep commons represented two horse commons or forty cow commons. The Proprietors changed these equations occasionally, which added to the confusion.

The system broke down when a few of the landowners became disgusted with the complicated arrangement and demanded that their shares be set off (awarded) to them individually. Most of the Proprietors opposed partition; they felt that dividing the common lands would ruin the sheep-raising industry. The dissidents were forced to sue, arguing that as common-law owners of common land, they were entitled to partition as a matter of right. The opposing Proprietors argued that under the peculiar wording of their charter from the Province of New York, the land was placed in trust to remain undivided forever. By the time this case reached the courts in 1813, the original twenty-seven shares had become subdivided into 2,000,000.

Faced with this monstrosity, it is no wonder that the court, in *Mitchell* v. *Starbuck*,[2] skirted the words of the islanders' charter and found that the owners of the land were tenants in common and were thus entitled to partition. Under this ruling, any owner of one hundred or more sheep commons could compel a division of his interest in one spot. Of course, the land was not uniform, and a solid block of sheep commons in a good location was worth a good deal more than single sheep commons scattered about the Island. Thus, the victors, Mitchell and his associates, turned in 2,886 sheep commons and received a set off of 2,100 acres in a Division known as Plainfield. This became known as "paying sheep commons for the land." These sheep commons were then canceled on the Proprietors' books, and the individual owners ceased to be Proprietors.

It was difficult to separate the common lands into individual ownership. As a result of the Mitchell case, Commissioners appointed by the court set off individual parcels to the winners in what became known as "The Great Set Off." Two of the three Commissioners were seamen, and they laid out the set offs or "allotted lands," as they were sometimes called, in a careless, ar-

[2] 10 Mass. 5 (1813).

bitrary manner. When Plainfield was awarded to Mitchell, the Proprietors bitterly complained that it was worth twice the value of any of the remaining common lands on the Island. This led to further litigation.

The set offs were usually made to groups of several owners, such as Mitchell and his associates. When these individual owners died, the lands were divided all over again by inheritance into common ownership. By the end of the nineteenth century, the "allotted lands" set off in 1821 were divided into almost as many infinitesimal shares as the common lands which remained in the Proprietorship.

Although Mitchell and his associates had won the right to set off their property in individually owned pastures, they lost one very important point which was to cause great trouble for the sheep industry. The court ruled that the roads running through the set offs were to be kept open for the use of the public forever. The owners of the newly set off "allotted lands" maintained their pastures unenclosed, just as the Proprietors had always done. Complaints that the sheep were blocking these public roads triggered "Nantucket's Sheep War."

In 1845 Nantucket's sheep industry entered its last legal tournament. The controversy came to a head when 900 sheep forced their way through the Town gates and bedded down in the Town Square every night. The streets ran with manure. In the mornings the shopkeepers along Main Street had to drive them away as even the sidewalks became choked with sheep.

Nantucket, like other towns in Massachusetts, was required by law to employ field drivers and pound keepers to deal with trespassing animals. The retribution of the Town was cruel. Hundreds of sheep were rounded up, placed in pounds and shamelessly neglected until they died of mistreatment, starvation, and thirst. The sheep owners retained Daniel Webster to sue the field drivers for their neglect, and the townspeople voted to indemnify the field drivers. Feelings grew even more bitter when it was discovered that the largest sheep owner on the Island didn't possess a single sheep common.

Litigation was prolonged, but before it terminated, its cause collapsed. Competition from the western states and from Australia destroyed the sheep industry. All activity ceased. The whaling industry was also dying, and the California Gold Rush of 1849 opened a new frontier for Nantucketers who migrated in droves, taking their wealth and even their ships with them.

Tristram Coffin's dream of a stable, sheep-raising community came to an end after having survived for almost two centuries. The moors were again deserted and have remained so until the present day. No more sheep-shearing festivals were held. The animals, whose wool and meat had preserved the islanders through the devastating blockades of the Revolution and the War of 1812, were gone, and with them went a large measure of the Island's prosperity. As a result, the outlying common lands became worthless, and few people bothered to keep track of their ownership. The landowners, who up until now had been so numerous, so vocal, and so litigious, simply faded away. The common lands reverted to that shadowy proprietorship known to the law as "Owners Unknown."

6
Pirates!

"Pirates!" yelled Nathan Skiff as he gazed helplessly at the red skeleton dancing on the huge black flag of the vessel bearing down on him. The rest of the crew aboard his little Nantucket whaling sloop froze in terror. They had felt secure on that sunny June day of 1723 whaling off the shoals eighty miles east of Nantucket, where pirates seldom surfaced.

But Ned Low was no ordinary pirate. He often popped up in unexpected places, and right now he was revenging himself on all "New England men." Moments before, his large vessel had been quietly ghosting by the sloop to weather, with no flags flying and only the helmsman on deck. Now Low's "Roger" suddenly broke out aloft. A hundred men lined the vessel's rail.

Skiff had only six whalers with him aboard the sloop, including two Indians and a boy. The rest of his crew were out in one of the sloop's whaleboats. His spine tingled with horror as he heard the pirate drummer beat to quarters and saw the swivel guns along the pirate's bulwarks trained upon him. Downwind, the men in the whaleboat had just harpooned a large whale and were being towed off on a Nantucket sleighride. Skiff desperately tried to signal them but, despite their preoccupation, they had already seen Low's Roger.

"Cut her loose!" bellowed the steersman. The boat fell backward at a right angle to the whale as oars flashed out through the thole pins. "Pull," ordered the steersman and the whaleboat took off toward another Nantucket whaling sloop, hulldown to the east'ard, leaving Skiff and the other six whalers behind to face the pirates.

The big vessel's sails flapped lazily in the light breeze as she drifted down on the sloop. The sea was so flat that the pirates grappled the sloop without a miss and stepped aboard as easily as if they had been stepping onto a dock.

"Where's the captain?" asked Ned Low, a small man with an air of great authority.

"Here, sir," said Skiff, stepping forward.

"Where do you hail from?" questioned Low.

"Nantucket, sir," Skiff replied.

Low studied the young man standing before him and a tense look of doubt passed over his brow. The look was gone instantly, and Low continued to stare at Skiff eyeball to eyeball. To Skiff, standing awkwardly before him, it seemed like an eternity before Low, in a calm voice, asked his third and final question.

"Are you married, lad?"

"No sir, not yet," answered Skiff in bewilderment.

"Then God help you," said Low, raising his cutlass and striking off Skiff's left ear. As blood began to run down Skiff's shoulder, the sight of it drove Low into an inexplicable fury. Yelling and cursing, he brought the cutlass down again and swiftly struck off Skiff's right ear. Still screaming at the top of his lungs, he beat Skiff over the head with the flat of the cutlass blade until the poor fellow was bathed in blood and his face was unrecognizable. Skiff collapsed on the deck in a pool of gore, and Low's rage evaporated as quickly as it had appeared.

"You've been a good lad," said Low, speaking as calmly as he had when he first boarded the sloop, "but, damn me, you're a New England man! The best I can do," he added softly, "is to reward you with an early death." With these words, he drew a cocked pistol out of his waistband and blew out Skiff's brains.

Meanwhile, the rest of the pirates had been looting the sloop. "Precious little here, Captain," reported the pirate quartermaster. "Enough blood spilt for one day, eh?"

Low agreed and decided to take the two Indians and the boy along with him as cabin boys. The rest of Skiff's crew were put in the sloop's remaining whaleboat with some biscuits and water and were permitted to row for Nantucket, where they arrived three days later.

Wasting no time, Low ordered his men to sink the sloop and to return to their own vessel. One by one the grappling hooks were freed up and their lines coiled down. The pirate vessel's blocks began to creak as her sheets were hove in, and she slowly started to move ahead of the sloop which was left sinking astern. In a matter of minutes, Nathan Skiff had become the first victim of Ned Low's capricious justice in what soon proved to be the bloodiest rampage to ever take place around Nantucket.

Ned Low was not the first pirate to appear in the area. In 1689 a pirate named Thomas Pound was captured in Vineyard Sound following a bloody sea battle off Tarpaulin Cove. Pound refused to strike his colors to a King's ship, after being told to do so, a serious offense under Admiralty law. He used his influential connections in Boston to win acquittal and eventually became the commander of a King's ship himself.

Piracy is said to be the third oldest profession, following prostitution and medicine. In many parts of the world pirates appeared before lawyers. Pirates first set foot on Nantucket in 1695, long before lawyers, when the crew of a French corsair landed at Squam Head.[1]

The Frenchmen plundered an outlying house, owned by the Bunker family and then forced the head of the household aboard the corsair to pilot them through Nantucket Sound. On the way, an English privateer engaged the corsair in a running sea fight while the anxious Nantucketers listened from the shore to the rumble of the cannonading. Following the fight, the Frenchmen dropped pilot Bunker off at Tarpaulin Cove, unscathed but thoroughly shaken up. From that day forward, he swore never to pilot pirates again, a job best left to the Admiralty Marshal.

The day's sail also cost Bunker a pretty penny. Tradition has it that, before departing, he buried all the family's gold so the pi-

[1] According to legal definition, a corsair is "a pirate ship sanctioned by the Country to which she belongs." A corsair differs from a privateer, which is a privately owned vessel specifically commissioned to seize, sink, or destroy enemy vessels, in that a corsair attacks the shipping of all countries except her own, at all times, whether there is a war in progress or not. The French sanctioned a number of corsairs based at Louisburg, Canada, which preyed on New England shipping.

rates wouldn't get it. But when he returned to Nantucket, he was so shaken up that he couldn't remember where he had hidden it. Generations of Bunkers since then have dug numerous holes about the Island, frantically seeking the family fortune; but, like most treasure hunters, they have never found a single penny.

Although Nantucket was sometimes plagued by pirates, she produced few, if any, of them. The islanders were sober, hard-working mariners who experienced enough excitement in the hazardous whaling industry. Paul Williams, reputedly born in Nantucket, is thought to be the only pirate captain ever to hail from the Island, and his career as a pirate was a comparatively undistinguished one.

Williams first went "on the account," the euphemism for turning pirate, with a partner named Bellamy. They operated a small flotilla of pirate ships. In April 1717 Bellamy had the misfortune of capturing an Irish pink loaded with wine off the Nantucket Shoals. The pirates transshipped the wine and, after overindulging as they often did, they were soon sailing around in circles. A spring line storm came in from the nor'east and the pirates steered a zigzag course up onto the sands of the outer Cape. One hundred forty-two pirates were drowned; their bodies littered the beaches. Seven survivors were apprehended on shore and marched from Cape Cod to the Boston jail. The only pirate to escape was a Cape Cod Indian named John Julian. He kept a low profile and simply faded away when his captors' backs were turned.

Although pirate gold covered the beaches of Wellfleet following the wreck, none of it ever entered the coffers of the Crown. An official sent down from Boston found it impossible to recover the gold from the hands of the canny Cape Codders who stonewalled him at every turn. Some of the pirates' gold coins are still floating around Boston today, in the hands of collectors.

Paul Williams did not share in the misfortune of his partner Bellamy. A few days earlier, he had become so inebriated on Block Island that he was incapable of following Bellamy to his doom. After sobering up, Williams took a short cruise through Nantucket Sound and disappeared. Even for a native-born Nantucketer, such as Williams, Nantucket's surrounding tide rips and shoals made it a forbidding spot. Pirates often sailed by the Island, but few of them ever landed or hovered about for long.

Williams and Bellamy proved to be bunglers, but Nantucketers were hard hit a few years later by the depredations of Ned Low. Pirates did not keep logs of their infamous deeds; most of Low's story has come down to us through the reminiscences of his unfortunate captives and the writings of ardent pirate buff Daniel Defoe.

Ned Low was born in London, near Westminster Abbey, in the closing years of the seventeenth century. When his younger brother turned seven, Ned began to lug the little fellow around London concealed in a shoulder basket. At a signal from Ned, the younger Low would pop up from his cover like a jack-in-the-box and snatch hats and wigs off the heads of unsuspecting victims. This routine required a wonderful sense of split-second timing, a talent which Ned Low was later to demonstrate time and again as a pirate.

On May 23, 1701, Captain Kidd was hanged at Wapping, between the high- and low-water marks, after having been tried by a jury and found guilty of piracy and murder.[2] All of London turned out for the show, including Ned Low and the brat in the basket. As the gaping spectators watched Kidd ascend the scaffold, young Low, snug in his basket, snatched a record number of greasy hats and wigs. The hanging itself turned out to be a spectacle which Ned Low would never forget.

For several days before the execution, an eager young minister had been chasing Kidd around, trying to get him to confess and repent. Kidd grew so fed up with these entreaties that on the

[2] The curious custom of hanging pirates between high and low water resulted from the ongoing battle for jurisdiction between the English courts. Lawyers, affected by the outcome, persuaded Parliament to pass the following statute limiting the Admiral's criminal jurisdiction to tidewater: "Never-the-less, of the death of a man and of a mayhem done in Great Ships being and hovering in the main streams of great rivers, only beneath the bridges of the same rivers nigh to the sea and in none other places of the same rivers the Admiral shall have cognizance."

Eventually this battle for jurisdiction between the competing courts narrowed down to the area between the mean high-water mark and the low-water mark. It was then held that when the tide was up, the place and the acts done upon it were within the jurisdiction of the Admiralty; when bare, being within the body of the country, the common law had jurisdiction. So it was here that the haughty English courts combined to send many a poor pirate to his doom.

day of the execution he got roaring drunk in an attempt to fend off the offensive minister. Despite this, the minister insisted on following him up the scaffold. The rope broke at the crucial moment, and Kidd went slithering into the seashore muck of Wapping. Not content with his previous exhortations, the minister continued to jabber at him as the half-conscious man was carried back up the scaffold and hanged a second time.

In accordance with Admiralty law, Kidd was chained to a post at the spot where he was executed until the tide had ebbed and flowed over his body three times. Then his body was tarred, bound in chains, and gibbeted at Tilbury Point for sailors in passing ships to observe. The thoroughness of the Admiralty law made a deep impression on Ned Low, who solemnly swore that he never would allow himself to be set up "a sun drying" like Captain Kidd.

Ned's brother in the basket was too young to get the message. When this little gudgeon grew too big for the basket and had to forgo the hat trick, he graduated to greater crimes. It wasn't long before the law claimed him. He ended his days on the scaffold at Tyburn.

Ned Low went to sea at an early age without ever having learned to read or write. After seeing the world for several years as a sailor, he arrived in Boston and married a girl from a reputable family on August 14, 1714. He settled down in Boston as a ship rigger, but his hot temper and quarrelsome disposition were good indications of the piratical turn his career would take. He could hardly have arrived in New England at a better moment for turning pirate; piracy thrived, unchecked, along the New England coast until 1730.

In 1719 Ned Low's young wife died, leaving him with a baby daughter, Elizabeth. He had been happily married and was devastated by his wife's untimely death, which cast him loose from his moorings and seems to have affected his sanity and in turn his subsequent actions as a pirate.

In 1721 Low was fired as a ship rigger and shipped out on a sloop bound for the Bay of Honduras. The purpose of the cruise was to pick up log wood and haul it back to Boston, which seems like an honest, Puritan occupation. But there were some legal objections to it: Honduras was owned by Spain, and the Bostonians were actually stealing the wood.

The Bay of Honduras was inhabited by retired pirates who had refused to accept pardons and instead had fled to this remote area to become log cutters. They were a rough lot, and the Bay was a rough place. Once in the Bay, the sloop sent in her long-boat, with the boat crew fully armed, to bring out the wood. It was tiring work and when the captain ordered an extra trip at the end of the day, Low, who had been in charge of lugging the wood, became furious and took a shot at him. The shot missed the captain but killed a sailor standing nearby. Low jumped in the longboat with some of his mates and took off. Pirates often began their careers in this fashion in the remote Caribbean, far from home, after having been pushed too far by their superior officers.

Once they got going "on the account" there was no reform-ing them as Captain John Smith, the first Admiral for New Eng-land, had pointed out. The next step was to trade up; transferring their guns and supplies to the bigger and faster ships they took along the way.

Low made his start in the right place. After eluding the Spanish Guarda Costas, he and his men captured a larger boat and joined forces with some other pirates. This enlarged force gave Low the opportunity to sail the circular pirate course of the era.

These pirate cruises were based on seasonal weather changes. First, in the spring, as the weather warmed up, the pi-rates would sail up the Carolina and Virginia coasts to the east-ern tip of Long Island, where they procured fresh water and supplies. Gardiners Island and Block Island were other favorite watering spots. Once their water casks were filled, the pirates would proceed to plunder ships sailing in and out of Newport. Then they would hover about in Vineyard Sound to catch coast-ing vessels moving east and west. Finally they would pass over the shoals at the eastern entrance to Nantucket Sound and pro-ceed to Nova Scotia and Newfoundland where they captured a number of fishing vessels and increased their crews.

At the end of the summer, they ran down to the Bahamas and then crossed the Atlantic, by way of the Azores, to the

Guinea Coast. From the Guinea Coast they recrossed the Atlantic to chase Portuguese shipping along the Brazilian Coast and then swung back to the Caribbean. Having successfully completed the circuit, they would end the winter refitting their ships and carousing until it was time to set sail again in the spring.

Ned Low managed to sail the course twice around, first in 1722 and again in 1723, without being captured. It was the conventional thing for reputable pirates to do, and yet the authorities never seemed to be able to cut them off. A fast cruiser patrolling the western end of Nantucket Sound in early summer could have bagged them every time.

Low started up the Atlantic Coast on May 28, 1722, in a brigantine armed with eight guns and carrying a pirate crew of forty-four men. Between Point Judith and Block Island he took his first prize, a small sloop, which he plundered and released. On the same day, he took a second sloop out of Newport. He cut away her bowsprit and removed her mainsail so she couldn't raise the alarm. Nevertheless, the disabled sloop made it into Block Island at midnight. A whaleboat was immediately dispatched to Newport with the news and pulled in the following morning at 7:00 A.M.

The Rhode Island Governor ordered the drums beaten for volunteers and two sloops were manned, one with ten guns and eighty men and the other, commanded by John Brown, Jr., with six guns and sixty men. The cautious Governor, afraid they might turn pirates themselves, gave the sloops only a ten-day commission for pirate chasing. They were on their way before sundown. The drum was also beaten in Boston, which sent out a large ship with one hundred men. The pirate brigantine could still be seen on the horizon off Block Island, but Low disappeared when the volunteer forces arrived, and they never even got a look at him before their commission expired.

The pirates had crept in amongst the Elizabeth Islands, which are almost as deserted today as they were in Low's time. The many passages between the islands and the strong currents surging through them made pirate chasing a difficult game. The high bluffs hid the pirates' masts and gave their lookouts a vantage point on their pursuers. Low's pursuers were nowhere in sight, and he set to work refilling his water casks and stealing sheep from the Elizabeth Islands and the nearby island of No Man's Land.

Low was active on the backside of the Vineyard. He plundered a small sloop there and began picking off small whaleboats operating inshore, crewed by Indians from Nantucket and Gay Head. Low kidnapped about half a dozen Indians and took them along with him when he left, passing over the shoals between Nantucket and Cape Cod and making for Roseway, Nova Scotia. On the run down, he amused himself by hanging two of the Indians from his yardarm for sport. The remainder, who could hardly speak English, he put to work as servants.

At Roseway, later renamed Shelbourne, Low captured a number of fishing vessels and swapped his brigantine for a newly built Marblehead schooner. Some of the younger fishermen he kidnapped or, as the expression then was, he "forced" them. The trick was to get these "forced men" to sign the ship's articles, which contained the guts of pirate law.

Low would have his big silver punch bowl filled with two gallons of rum and brandy and placed in the captain's cabin. He would then invite the forced men to his cabin to join him in a drink, at the same time trying to wheedle them into signing the articles. Even if they were brave enough to refuse to sign, the poor captives were still in a tenuous legal position. Nobody believed the forced men when a pirate ship was captured, and they were often hanged along with the pirates. The predicament of the poor Indians who knew nothing of English law, pirate law, or international law and who barely spoke English was the worst of all.

The only hope for the forced men was to advertise in the newspaper. This was done for them by their comrades who escaped or were released. These former shipmates would go before a notary public and swear that their unfortunate mates still aboard the pirate ship had been forced. This affidavit was then inserted in the local newspaper and was admissible at any future trial. Of course, every man from a captured pirate ship swore on the Bible that he had been forced, so pirate trials usually boiled down to separating the true captives from the fakers.

Low pressed on to Newfoundland, where he had no difficulty persuading captured fishermen to sign the articles.

Newfoundland was always a good recruiting ground for pirates because the people there lived such a harsh existence. After a winter surviving on "black strap," a fish chowder made with rum and beer, the Newfoundlanders were ready to sign up for anything.[3]

On Low's run in 1722, he took many vessels without doing much fighting. At the end of nineteen months, he had taken 134 prizes, which was a new record for a New England pirate. Most of these vessels were captured off Newfoundland and the Grand Banks.

From Newfoundland, Low doubled back to Nova Scotia, where he learned that a large man-of-war was out after him. He decided to make the run south to the Leeward Islands in the Marblehead schooner and a recently captured French banker. On this passage, undertaken in the late summer, the pirates ran into one of the worst West Indian hurricanes on record.

The pirates were forced to throw their guns and supplies overboard. They pumped and even bailed with buckets as both vessels started to founder. Just as they were about to cut away the French banker's masts, they got ahead of the leaks and were able to save her masts by rigging preventer stays. The schooner blew out her mainsail, lost both anchors and damaged her bowsprit. Low took them for refitting to a small, remote island where they traded their remaining supplies with the natives, before continuing across the Atlantic to the Azores, where they began to pick up one prize after another.

In the Azores, an event occurred which was to have repercussions off Nantucket. The pirates captured a ship carrying three hundred gallons of brandy, and Low became a confirmed alcoholic. Although Low was a brutal man who developed an irrational hatred for his fellow New Englanders, he did have one soft spot. He made it his invariable practice never to harm a married man, and he used to get a crying jag whenever he was reminded of his little daughter growing up in Boston.

Low, a small man, was able to stay on top of his unruly pirate crew—apparently by the sheer terror he inspired in his con-

---

[3] Apparently, black strap was less invigorating than today's Le Celebre Screech de Terre-Neuva, a dark rum which the Newfoundland Liquor Corporation imports from Jamaica.

temporaries. As his deeds became increasingly bloody, no one dared oppose him except the ship's doctor. Once, after Low's jaw had been sliced in a fight and the doctor was sewing it up, Low found fault with the doctor's work.

"Well, if you don't like it, take that!" snapped the doctor, throwing a punch which tore out all the stitches he had just put in. Low quickly retired to his cabin with his brandy bottle, which was possibly the only time in his career as a pirate that he was ever put down.

As the winter of 1723 drew to a close, Low returned to the Bay of Honduras, the point from which he had started his cruise. As usual, a fleet of New England vessels was there stealing wood. In the midst of their activities, the Spanish ships of the Guarda Costas arrived and captured all the New Englanders. Hoisting a Spanish flag to confuse the issue, Low sailed in and captured both the Guarda Costas and the New Englanders. He released the New Englanders after clipping their ears, while his crew killed most of the Spaniards.

All was now ready for the summer cruise, and Low decided to repeat the course he had sailed so successfully in 1722. In May he started up the Carolina and Virginia coasts in command of the sloop *Fortune,* accompanied by his cohort, a Captain Harris, who commanded the sloop *Ranger.* Besides an ample supply of brandy, low was reputed to have been carrying £150,000 worth of gold, silver, and plate in the *Fortune,* so the cruise was apparently not undertaken out of necessity but only to keep professionally occupied. The pirates captured sixteen vessels as they traveled north.

These pirates were desperate men who well knew the risks they were running. Even Low had reservations about going up a rope and perhaps coming down again in the muck between high and low water, if the New Englanders were too cheap to provide decent hemp. Kidd's hanging had been a sufficient example, and Low vowed suicide rather than surrender to the Admiralty Marshal. All these gray thoughts sent the pirates scurrying for their brandy bottles and increased their brutality on their unfortunate captives.

Cruising safely offshore, the pirate fleet continued along the coast until they spied a large prize off the eastern tip of Long Island and chased after her. The prize turned out to be the *Greyhound,* a warship of twenty guns and one hundred twenty men, commanded by a Captain Solgard, which had been sent out to capture the pirates.

The wind lightened and the pirates, realizing their mistake, tried to row away. Although the *Greyhound* was a big ship to row, Captain Solgard put eighty-six men on the oars and eventually overtook the pirates. He forced his way between their two vessels and shot a large hole in Low's rigging. This was too much for Low, and he sneaked away from the fight, leaving Harris to be captured.

Ten or twelve of Harris's men had been killed and the rest, discouraged by Low's flight, yelled for quarter. One of these pirates attempted to blow up the *Ranger.* Frustrated in his attempt, he rushed forward, seized a pistol, and blew his brains out. Thirty-seven whites, six blacks, and one of the Indians who had been forced off Nantucket the year before were taken and put in irons. Solgard unsuccessfully pursued Low, who disappeared over the northeast horizon. Giving up the chase, Solgard sailed into Newport with his prisoners.

Low went berserk at the loss of Harris and took his revenge on the defenseless Nantucket whaling fleet operating about 80 miles offshore. Two days after his run-in with the *Greyhound,* he claimed Nathan Skiff as his first victim. Nobody knows how many vessels he destroyed on this rampage because he often sank them after killing their entire crews.

A couple of days after he killed Skiff, Low took a fishing vessel between Nantucket and Block Island. He cut the captain's head off with his cutlass and turned the captured boat over to the murdered man's crew of two Indians, telling them that he intended to kill the master of every New England vessel he encountered. The terrified Indians soon carried the message ashore. That same afternoon, Low captured another fishing sloop. He ripped out the captain's heart while the poor man was still alive and ordered it roasted. Then he forced the vessel's mate to eat the roasted heart.

Next Low took a number of whaling sloops and made the

captains eat their own ears sprinkled with salt and pepper. Finally, the other pirates revolted at this senseless bloodshed and Low squared away for Canada, unscathed by the forces sent out to catch him.

One of the sloops Low must have boarded was found abandoned off Nantucket with her sails flapping and an empty wine cask on deck. Apparently he had killed everyone on board and thrown the corpses into the sea. This sloop was towed to Boston by the finder, who filed a claim for salvage against her in the Vice Admiralty Court.

When the *Greyhound* first arrived in Newport with her prisoners, New England went wild with excitement. At this time, practically every New Englander lived within thirty or forty miles of tidewater and they all depended on the sea for their livelihoods, in one way or another. Never had so many pirates been taken at one time.

James Franklin, the printer of the New England *Courant*, saw a chance to sell a lot of newspapers and reported that the, Massachusetts General Court was fitting out a large vessel to go after Low. Whatever the General Court was planning, they didn't want Low or the general public to get wind of it, and they jailed Franklin for "a high affront to this government" until the legislative session was completed. Luckily for Franklin, legislative sessions of the Massachusetts General Court were shorter then than they are now. Like his grandfather, Peter Folger, the unfortunate printer was lugged off to jail for contempt in an age before Freedom of the Press was championed and the public had its right to know. In his absence, the *Courant* continued to operate under the management of the printer's younger brother, Ben Franklin, who was only a boy at the time.

About three weeks after the pirates were captured, various members of the Vice Admiralty Court, led by Lieutenant Governor William Dummer of Massachusetts, the President of the Court, rode down on horseback from Boston to Newport for the trial. Governor Samuel Cranston of Rhode Island also served on this Court, which included various other high officials of the Crown.

As this was an American Vice Admiralty Court trial, there

was no indictment by a Grand Jury and trial by a Petty Jury, as there had been in the case of Captain Kidd.[4] Articles alleging piracy and robbery were drawn up by the prosecution. The Vice Admiralty Court organized itself in the evening, and then its members went out and enjoyed a hearty dinner.

At eight the next morning, the members solemnly filed into court led by the Admiralty Marshal carrying a three-foot-long silver oar, his badge of office, which he laid on the bench before the judges.[5] This dreaded official had custody of the pirates, who referred to him as "the man with the silver oar." The mention of his name threw them into paroxysms of fear.

Under the trial procedure of that time, defendants were allowed to be represented by counsel only on points of law. Defense counsels were not permitted to cross-examine witnesses. At this trial, none of the defendants were represented by counsel. All of them pleaded not guilty and alleged that they were forced men, held on the pirate vessel against their will.

Thomas Mumford, the Indian defendant, was in a particularly difficult position because he spoke little English. With no lawyer to defend him, he appeared to be at the mercy of the Court. Excitement heightened when Abishai Folger arrived from Nantucket to act as his interpreter.

After the prisoners were arraigned, they were divided into groups to stand trial. One or two of the pirates had already died in jail of their wounds. The first batch of prisoners consisted of fourteen men who were placed on trial immediately following their arraignment.

The Advocate General for the King gave the opening speech to the Court and outlined the crime of piracy:

> This sort of criminals are engaged in a perpetual war
> with every individual, with every state, Christian and

[4] Defendants were denied the right to jury trials in the Vice Admiralty Courts established in America, a grievance stated in our Declaration of Independence.

[5] This emblem of the Admiralty Court was already centuries old. The oldest silver oar is that of the Cinque Ports, presently preserved at Dover Castle. The silver oar of the English High Court in Admiralty comes from the Tudor period, and the blade is inscribed with anchors and the Royal Coat of Arms. For years, arresting officers of the Court carried miniature silver oars, and Admiralty Court officers wore silver oar pins. An old wooden oar of the United States Admiralty Marshal is currently preserved at the Federal Court in Boston.

infidel, they have no Country, but by the nature of their guilt, separate themselves, renouncing the benefit of all lawful society to commit heinous crimes. The Romans, therefore, justly styled them Hostes humani generis, enemies of mankind and indeed they are enemies and armed. . . .

As the Advocate General's case went on, it began to look worse and worse for the defendants. In the courtroom sat a merchant captain with an ear clipped off, together with other former captives who were able to identify the pirates and describe their criminal acts. The telltale marks of a true pirate were: (1) signing the ship's articles, (2) being in harness (wearing a sword belt or carrying a cutlass or pistol) during an action; (3) sharing in the plunder.

Thomas Mumford was tried with the second batch of prisoners. With the help of Abishai Folger, who was sworn in as interpreter, he haltingly gave the following testimony: "I was a servant a fishing last year, and was taken out of a fishing sloop with five Indians off of Nantucket by Low and company, and they hanged two of us at Cape Sable and I was kept by Low ever since and had about six bitts on me when I was taken."

After each batch of prisoners was tried, the Court filed out to vote a verdict but returned immediately, hardly taking the time to sit down. Dummer, as President of the Court, pronounced findings of guilty on the pirates and sentenced them to be hanged by the neck until dead.

Few defendants went free. Two pirates were recommended "unto his Majesty for Remission." Thomas Mumford and a fifteen-year-old boy were the only defendants in the second batch who were found not guilty.

Although he had been found not guilty, Thomas Mumford's part in the sorry affair was not yet over. The third and final batch of prisoners contained Thomas Powell, the gunner of the pirate sloop, along with Joseph Libbey and Joseph Sweetser. Libbey and Sweetser both produced legal notices their shipmates had printed in the newspapers to prove that they were forced men. Mumford was put back on the stand to determine whether these three men were really forced as they claimed or whether they were pirates.

With Folger's help, Mumford gave the following testimony:

> I saw Powell have a gun when they took vessels, but I never saw him fire; I saw him go on board of a vessel once, but he brought nothing from her that I saw; I saw him once shoot a Negro but never a white man.
>
> I saw Joseph Libbey once go aboard a captured vessel and bring back a pair of stockings.
>
> Joseph Sweetser cooked it on board with me sometimes and sometimes they made him hand the sails; once I saw Sweetser clean a gun, but not fire it, and Sweetser once told me he wanted to get ashore from among them and he said if the man-of-war should take them they would hang him, and in the fight with the *Greyhound* I saw Sweetser sitting unarmed in the range of the sloop's mast and sometime before the fight I heard him ask Low to let him have his liberty and go ashore, but he was refused.

As a result of Mumford's testimony, Powell and Libbey were found guilty and Sweetser was cleared. This concluded the work of the Vice Admiralty Court in the courtroom, although the members usually attended the executions. The Newport population now prepared everything for the executions which it had known from the beginning were sure to follow.

Pirate executions at that time were big events, attended by thousands of people. First the minister went to the condemned, urging them to confess and repent. Then the pirates were paraded through the streets to the place of execution, accompanied by a strong guard. The parade was led by the Admiralty Marshal carrying his silver oar, followed by the officials and ministers. At the place of execution, between high and low water, the condemned were encouraged to give final speeches, confessing their misdeeds and warning the spectators of the wages of sin.

At the Newport hangings, John Fitz-Gerald, the only Irishman in the pirate crew, did himself proud composing a little

poem for the occasion which he recited to the crowd. The con-
cluding stanza went:

I pray the Lord preserve you and keep you from this End;
O let Fitz-Gerald's great downfall unto your welfare tend.
I to the Lord my Soul bequeath, accept thereof I pray,
My Body to the Earth bequeath, dear Friend, adieu for aye.

The executions took place on July 19, 1723, at noon.
Ben Franklin gave the following description of the event in
the New England *Courant:*

Mr. Bass went to Prayer with them; and some little time
after, the Rev. Mr. Clap concluded with a short exhorta-
tion to them. Their Black Flag with the Pourtrature of
Death having an Hour-glass in one Hand and a Dart in
the other, at the end of which was the Form of a Heart
with three drops of Blood, falling from it, was affix'd at
one corner of the Gallows. This flag they call'd Old
Roger, and often us'd to say they would live and die
under it.

After the pirates had emitted their dying moans, their bodies
were cut down and buried between the high- and low-water
marks at Goat Island in Newport Harbor. In this instance, none
of them was gibbeted at the harbor's entrance for the seamen of
passing ships to observe. Apparently, this procedure was being
reserved for the capture of Ned Low, the colonies' public enemy
number one.

Many reports of Ned Low's capture began to come to hand
and were dutifully reported in the *Courant.* He had been taken
off Nova Scotia, the Azores, the African Coast, the Brazilian
Coast, and in the West Indies. Actually, Low had taken the
Merry Christmas, a thirty-four-gun ship, and was sailing around
at the head of an enlarged pirate fleet. Low, always a man of big
ideas, styled himself "Admiral."

Still the rumors of Low's capture persisted, but he took a
New England ship in the Barbadoes in the spring of 1724, which
shows that he had completed the course a second time and was

still active. Some say that his crew revolted at all his bloody deeds and marooned him, the traditional pirate punishment. Others say that he was taken by a French cruiser and strung up even faster than British justice would have allowed. Still others say that he escaped among the Mosquito Indians. Perhaps it was the brandy that got him in the end.

For a generation afterward, Nantucket children used to quake under their patchwork quilts on stormy nights after being told stories about this bloodthirsty pirate. But for one reason or another he never did make it back to New England for a third run. Ned Low fulfilled the vow he had made in London years before. He never permitted himself to be piloted up the scaffold by "the man with the silver oar."

7

Evil Be to Those
Who Evil Think

After the disastrous years of the American Revolution, an increased international demand for whale oil brought prosperity back to Nantucket. The Island's economy revived, and its population grew to 5,000, most of whom were engaged in the enterprise of whaling. As Nantucketer Walter Folger, Jr., described his community: "The inhabitants live together like one great family, not in one house, but in friendship. They not only know their nearest neighbors but each one knows the rest."

To meet the needs of the growing whale-oil business, the islanders, with the help of some wealthy Boston merchants, founded one of the first banks in the United States. It was called the Nantucket Bank and was incorporated by an act of the legislature. Its capital stock of $40,000 was to be paid for in installments by its shareholders, and it was to be governed by twelve directors. The Nantucket Bank opened its doors for business on lower Main Street in June 1795.

The new bank immediately became an object of suspicion. One Nantucketer, who was tendered a personal check drawn on the bank, was slow to comprehend that the check represented money. He took it home and talked it over with his family, who also failed to understand it. After turning it over again and again and thoroughly examining the front and the back, he concluded darkly: "It is a check; it is deviltry. I want nothing of it." And, so saying, he threw it in the fire. The islanders had always obtained credit from their neighbors, and they didn't understand banks— nor did they see the need for one. In an age when superstition and a fear of the supernatural played a large part in everyday affairs, many Nantucketers soon figured out that the bank was the work of the Devil.

At this time, three-fourths of the islanders were members of the Quaker Meeting and the Island was run by the Quaker elders. Quakerism had fostered industry and morality on the Island, but by 1795 many of the elders, tied to old customs, had become narrow-minded and autocratic. Members were read out of the Meeting for trivial offenses, such as wearing shoe buckles or wigs. All music, fashion, and scientific study were forbidden. As a result, some of the younger men in town rebelled against the tyranny of the elders.

The violent birth of the two-party system in America gave rise to fierce political rivalries on Nantucket. Oddly enough, the Quakers, who were the old ruling order on the Island, joined the new Jeffersonian Democratic Party, while the newer men remained with the conservative Federalist Party. The Quaker Meeting was rapidly falling apart over trivial disputes, but the older Quakers still ran the Island with an iron hand, guided by their "inner light." They resented any encroachment by upstarts and outsiders whom they termed "world's people." Under these conditions, the new bank got off to an uneasy start. Although it was run mainly by the old-guard Quakers, some of its directors and personnel were members of the new, rebellious faction.

Locks of any kind had never been used on Nantucket and had always been viewed as a needless expense because of the absence of crime in the small, tightly knit community. However, the bank directors, as prudent men, took precautions to secure the bank. They constructed a series of locked doors leading to the vault. The vault door itself was stoutly secured by a new "off-set" lock purchased in Boston and thought to be foolproof.

Early on the morning of June 22, 1795, the bank's cashier, Randall Rice, stopped to chat with his merchant friend, Joseph Nichols, before opening the bank promptly at 8:45. Randall Rice was a native of Rhode Island who had married a Nantucket girl and moved to the Island, where he was a part-time lawyer, butcher, and real estate speculator. He was a member of the rebellious new faction which was trying to wrest economic and political power out of the hands of the old Nantucket Quakers. The Quakers resented him as an outsider and looked down on him as one of the "world's people."

Rice unlocked the final off-set lock on the vault and noticed that it was particularly hard to open. He then went to the nearest specie chest to get out the day's operating funds. Fear seized him instantly when he saw that it was empty. He quickly examined other specie chests and found them empty too. The bank had been robbed of a total of $22,000—an enormous sum in those days, and $8,000 more than the amount which had been paid on the installments of the capital stock.

Rice immediately met with the bank directors. It was decided to withhold news of the robbery until the end of the week. The delay of the news led to the charge that two of the directors had withdrawn the money to corner that year's whale-oil market, intending to replace it before the loss was discovered. Actually, William Coffin and Albert Gardner, the two suspected bank directors, had formed an oil-buying syndicate shortly before the robbery; but after the robbery, the syndicate was abandoned before it ever purchased any oil. Both men were members of the new faction. Coffin was the Postmaster of Nantucket, appointed by the Federalists, and Gardner was a trading-sloop captain.

The specie taken consisted of gold crowns, silver dollars, French coins, and Spanish pistoles. It was tremendously heavy, and its complete disappearance in one night added to the mystery. The Island was searched, but none of the money was ever recovered. The only clue was a greasy handkerchief belonging to Randall Rice which was found in the vault. Although Coffin and Gardner remained suspects, Rice became the prime suspect and the central figure in the drawn-out prosecution which followed.

Rivalry, jealousy and personal hatred produced a rash of other accusations. With no clues to pursue, the islanders resorted to physiognomy (a popular "science" which claimed that a man's character and deeds could be determined by his facial expressions), astrology, dreams, and gossip to produce suspects. They deserted their shops and milled about the street in a mood of hysteria. In such an atmosphere, rational inquiry gave way to prejudice and the Quaker bank directors, acting as vigilantes, began to arrest suspects.

Today such behavior by private citizens would be illegal, but in those days of few police, jails, or district attorneys, criminal prosecutions were often initiated and carried out by private parties. The aggrieved citizen had to do much of his own police work and prosecute suspects through privately hired attorneys. The state provided only law courts and a few porous jails.

The first suspect arrested was Randall Rice. His prosecutors had a piece of evidence far more damaging than his handkerchief, found in the vault. Rice had been feuding with Walter Folger, Sr. On the day of the robbery, they passed each other in the street, and Rice "sheered off" to avoid him. Folger, an ardent physiognomist, determined that Rice's actions were furtive; and later that same morning, upon being informed of the robbery, he immediately accused Rice. Folger was a prominent citizen so his opinion was given great weight and became evidence against Rice.

Rice's friend, Joseph Nichols, owned the store adjoining the bank. As it was obvious that Rice could not possibly have robbed the bank without help, Joseph Nichols and his son were also arrested and held incommunicado by a band of Quaker bank directors and stockholders. After a hearing before the Justice of the Peace, all three suspects were released for lack of evidence. Joseph Nichols, however, was removed as Clerk of Courts and never reinstated. The records of these proceedings were removed by unknown persons and never returned, adding another element of mystery to the bank robbery.

On August 25, 1795, the bank's President, Joseph Chase, retained an astrologer in Providence to solve the crime. The astrologer said that four Nantucketers had committed the robbery. The descriptions he gave fitted the two suspected bank directors, William Coffin and Albert Gardner, the Judge of Probate, Jethro Hussey, and Samuel Barker. In August a federal marshal, sent down from Boston, ransacked the house of an eighth suspect, Josiah Barker, but nothing was found.

In September nationally famous lawyers from Boston arrived on the Island, and a special Court of Inquiry was convened.

James Prescott, Jr., a promising young jurist, presided.[1] This was
the first major appearance of professional lawyers on Nantucket.
Samuel Dexter, Jr., Boston's leading trial lawyer, prosecuted the
case on behalf of the bank President and a majority of the directors. Dexter was related through his mother, Hannah Sigourney,
to the Nantucket Barkers, some of the very people he was
prosecuting. Most of the antagonists in the bank robbery case
were related, and this made the hatreds all the more bitter and
lasting. Harrison Grey Otis appeared for the defendants. He had
a national reputation as the leading Federalist of the era, and his
appearance clearly showed that the bank robbery case had become a political trial.

One of the main prosecution witnesses was William Worth.
Despite the fact that the night of the robbery had been extremely
foggy, Worth had testified at the earlier hearing before the Justice of the Peace that he had been standing on a nearby wharf
and had actually seen Randall Rice and Joseph Nichols enter the
bank. This testimony was corroborated in part by two other prosecution witnesses.

Now Worth recanted, confessed that he had lied and admitted that he had not been near the bank the night it was robbed.
The story of the second prosecution witness collapsed because he
had sworn before the Justice of the Peace that he had seen Worth
near the bank. The story of the third prosecution witness also fell
apart because she had testified that she had overheard Rice and
another man say that they were afraid Worth had seen them
enter the bank. All three prosecution witnesses were immediately
arrested and held on perjury charges.

The prosecution forces recovered themselves quickly. Otis,
the defendants' attorney, was staying at a Nantucket boarding
house run by Peggy Pinkham. Peggy stationed herself at a
keyhole and heard Otis going over the case with his clients.
Peggy was then rushed onto the stand by the prosecution and
testified to incriminating statements supposedly made by the defendants to Otis.

[1] Years after the Nantucket Bank robbery, Prescott achieved the dubious
distinction of being the first judge impeached and disbarred in Massachusetts.
Most of the charges against him involved bribery, and he was always suspected
of having been bribed in the bank robbery case.

Other Nantucketers had had dreams which coincided with the pronouncements of the Providence astrologer. The contents of these dreams, together with the opinion of the astrologer, were all admitted into evidence at the inquiry. Apparently, Judge Prescott completely disregarded the rules of evidence.

At the conclusion of the hearing, Randall Rice, Judge Jethro Hussey, and Samuel Barker were held for the Grand Jury and released on bail of $21,600 each. Randall Rice couldn't afford bail, and he was jailed for many months before his brother finally put up the money. Rice was a man of modest means with a wife and seven young children to support. He borrowed in all directions, including mortgaging his property, in order to raise money for his defense.

In February 1796 the Quaker prosecutors managed to get legislation passed transferring the case to the Supreme Judicial Court sitting in Boston. This meant that the bank robbery defendants would be indicted and tried by Suffolk County jurors in Boston, who were more apt to indict and convict them than Nantucket jurors, who had personal knowledge of the circumstances.

In September 1796 almost one hundred Nantucketers appeared before the Suffolk County Grand Jury either as defendants, witnesses, or interested parties. No indictments were returned on any of the charges, including the perjury charges against the three erring prosection witnesses.

By this time the stockholders had replenished the bank's depleted capital and it was managing to stay afloat. If wisdom had prevailed, the whole matter would have been dropped for lack of evidence at this point, a little over a year after the robbery. Instead, the defendants demanded satisfaction, and they foolishly insisted on suing their prosecutors for malicious prosecution and slander.

Bank Director Albert Gardner sued Captain Uriah Swain for accusing him of being a bank robber and lost. Randall Rice got into a fistfight on the Nantucket docks which ended with two hundred angry men sparring with each other. A rash of other fistfights resulted in a series of assault-and-battery cases, most of which were disposed of through arbitration. Having brought their opponents into court, the Nantucketers preferred settling matters among themselves rather than submitting them to the judgment of outsiders.

Randall Rice, however, sued Walter Folger, Sr., in the Barnstable Court for malicious prosecution. Numerous depositions were taken on Nantucket, and the cost of transferring the case to the mainland was enormous. Rice lost the case and Folger was awarded $5,000 costs, which would have wiped out Rice. Rice appealed the case to Boston and finally won ten dollars' damages. Folger was so enraged at ultimately losing his case that he reopened the bank robbery prosecution, setting the stage for the final act of the tragedy.

Dexter remained the chief prosecution lawyer. Fisher Ames took over from Otis for the defense. Like Otis, he was an arch-Federalist who had achieved a national reputation in Congress as an orator. The newly discovered evidence which triggered the second prosecution was, again, a supposedly overheard conversation between Rice and his lawyer.

As the conflict widened, more and more people were drawn into the fray. Many Nantucketers moved from the Island rather than take sides. Many of those who stayed behind were not on speaking terms with one another.

The second Grand Jury hearing was held at Boston in August 1797. Randall Rice, Judge Hussey, and Samuel Barker were again defendants. This time the two suspected bank directors, William Coffin and Albert Gardner, were added as defendants. In addition to his other activities, Coffin ran a wig-making shop where the young men of the town would gather and discuss the overthrow of the Quaker regime. Wigs were especially offensive to the simple tastes of the Quakers, who were determined to squelch Coffin. Albert Gardner was Coffin's best friend.

In this second round, the prosecution finally prevailed, and all five defendants were indicted. Apparently, the Boston Grand Jury was impressed by the fifty-two Nantucket witnesses whom the prosecution paraded before them. The trial took place a few days after the indictments, before a Boston jury with Robert Treat Paine, a signer of the Declaration of Independence, presiding.

Rice's principal witness was deathly ill on Nantucket and

couldn't appear. The prosecution's evidence was as slight as it had always been. In closing, Fisher Ames harangued the jury on behalf of the defendants for four straight hours without a break. The defendants sat back to await the verdict, convinced that they would soon be vindicated.

Sure enough, the defendants were found not guilty—all, that is, except poor Randall Rice who was found guilty and returned to jail. Judgment was stayed until February 1798, and Rice was held in $60,000 bail. Of course, he couldn't raise this amount, and he remained in jail in Boston while all of his property on Nantucket was foreclosed. Meanwhile, his brother, who had helped furnish the bail for the first prosecution, died.

No evidence was ever introduced that Rice had ever possessed or disposed of the money. Moreover, it would have been physically impossible for him to have moved such a great load of coins without help. The only shred of evidence against him was that his greasy butcher's handkerchief had been found in the vault. After all, he was the bank's cashier with every right to be in the vault. Probably he had innocently dropped it there. The tide of feeling on Nantucket began to turn strongly in Rice's favor, but, it was too late: the Boston jury verdict could not be upset.

Judge Paine felt that Rice was innocent and postponed entering judgment. Rice remained in the Boston jail during 1798. His wife was reduced to poverty, and his infant son died while he was in jail. In June 1798 he petitioned the legislature for a new trial. Unfortunately for him, Nantucket's State Representative at this time was Micajah Coffin, a stern old Quaker who had spearheaded the prosecution. Micajah was an influential member of the House and, due to his violent opposition, the petition was denied.

Since the robbery in 1795, the prosecuted faction, who knew themselves to be innocent, had been trying to catch the real bank robbers. When the money failed to turn up on Nantucket, they began to suspect off-islanders, and they made many trips to the mainland in search of the real thieves. Letters were sent to all the principal cities on the East Coast, and soon these efforts began to bear fruit.

In February 1796 a suspect named Zeb Withers, alias Weatherly, was apprehended in Philadelphia. He was released for lack of evidence and fled to New Haven. A Nantucket sea captain pursued him to New Haven and brought him back in irons for questioning. The captain soon reappeared on Nantucket with a second prisoner, John Clark, Jr., whom he had seized in New York. The two prisoners promptly confessed to having played a part in the robbery and implicated another accomplice, Sam Johnson.

Despite these confessions, the prosecution of Randall Rice and the other defendants had rolled on. Elisha Sigourney, a Boston merchant and a large stockholder in the bank, wrote a friend on Nantucket:

> The late discovery of the real robbers of our Bank must
> be very sensibly felt by you and all our suffering friends
> —what part the conjurers, the dreamers and liars will
> take I cannot prophecy but if they act as I would ad-
> vise, they will forsake their deeds of darkness and con-
> fess their folly—for my mind is fully convinced the rob-
> bers are Johnson, Withers and Clark, Jr. and it will
> come to light.

On Nantucket a vigilante committee of Quaker bank directors kept Withers and Clark under guard. This committee was obsessed with the idea of linking the two self-confessed, off-island robbers with their fellow Nantucketers. Public opinion forced the vigilantes to transfer the suspects to the Nantucket jail, where Daniel Kelley was assigned to guard them. Kelley obtained more detailed confessions from them about the looting of the bank but they did not implicate any Nantucketers.

After a month of confinement, the prisoners escaped. They hid in ropewalks by night and swamps by day until they stole a lifeboat and rowed to the mainland. Their confessions were never introduced at Rice's trial. The Quaker faction was so intent on convicting their rivals that it is probable they permitted the prisoners to escape and suppressed their confessions.

Albert Gardner would not give up. After his acquittal in late

1797, he sailed straight to New York and captured the heavily armed Withers right on the city streets. This time Gardner lodged Withers in the Boston jail. Amazingly, Withers found himself in a cell next to the convicted bank robber Randall Rice. The bewildered jury which had convicted Rice, on learning about Withers, began to intercede for Rice but, before anything could be done, Withers escaped a second time.

It was at this time that Rice petitioned the legislature for a new trial and was turned down. Randall Rice saw his last hope of vindication slip away. Although he steadfastly refused to petition for a pardon, his friends eventually convinced him to do so. The prosecutors, represented by Dexter, firmly opposed the move, but in December 1798 he was pardoned by the Governor and released from jail.

Rice returned to Nantucket where he attempted to practice law, but was soon jailed for the debts he had accumulated while he was confined in Boston. Rice was never indemnified for the wrongs he had suffered, and he was unable to get back on his feet again after his Boston imprisonment. He died within ten years, an impoverished and ruined man.

Years later, Withers, who was in jail in New York for unrelated crimes, told the whole story of the robbery to William McFate, a fellow prisoner. Withers died in prison, and McFate related the story to the prison agent, Nantucket-born Alex Coffin, who in turn relayed it to William Coffin and Albert Gardner on Nantucket. In 1816, twenty-one years after the robbery, Coffin and Gardner published an account of the robbery, showing that no Nantucketer had been involved; but it still failed to convince many of their enemies. This is the story they told:

On the weekend of the robbery, Captain John Clark, Jr., Zeb Withers, and Sam Johnson sailed into Nantucket on the *Dolphin*, a trading sloop out of New Haven. All three had criminal records in the New Haven area, where Captain Clark's father ran a thieves' market. The operation consisted of stealing goods in one port and selling them in another. The junior Clark had made many trips to Nantucket, where the islanders liked his cut-rate prices. The bargains were a tip-off to the kind of trader he was, but Clark was an engaging rogue who kept the local merchants amused with his stories as he sold off his cargoes of fenced goods. They obligingly closed their eyes to any suspicions.

In the course of his visits, Clark learned about the new bank and devised a plan to rob it. On the weekend of the robbery, after selling his goods, Clark told everyone that his business was completed and he was going to sail back to the mainland. Instead, he anchored far out in the harbor. A heavy fog hid his sloop from the islanders, who believed it had already set sail for the mainland. After everyone had gone to bed, Clark and his crew rowed back to the wharf with muffled oars.

Once ashore, the men skillfully set to work. While the junior member stood guard outside in the pea-soup fog, Clark and Withers took wax impressions of the locks and whittled pewter spoons into the shape of keys. All went smoothly until they came to the final off-set lock on the vault door. Withers was an accomplished safecracker but the off-set proved too much for his expertise.

Clark, however, refused to give up. He had heard somewhere that the new off-sets were hard to pick but that they were brittle. Deciding that the glittering prize was great enough to hazard some noise, he inserted his sailor's knife in the lock and swung a pistol butt against it in one decisive stroke. The blow rang out like a pistol shot, but no one appeared out of the fog. The off-set gave way, and the thieves entered the vault. They proceeded to loot the bank, filling sacks they found in the vault with the coins and carrying them down to the wharf and the waiting skiff.

The operation had taken all night. As the robbers hoisted sail a morning breeze sprang up, dispersing the fog and speeding them on their way. The robbers buried their loot at various deserted points along the shores of Long Island and began to enjoy their newly acquired treasure undisturbed. No part of the money was ever recovered by the bank, and, with the exception of the brief imprisonments of Clark and Withers, the trio escaped any punishment for their crime.

The Great Bank Robbery devastated Nantucket and marked a significant turn in the Island's history. More shocking to the town than the robbery itself were the displays of venom, violence, and vindictiveness which swept the community. The fights between the early settlers had divided families and alienated neighbors, but the community had recovered. The wounds left by the bank robbery never healed. Gone forever was the dream of sharing common lands and common endeavors.

In June 1805, exactly ten years after the bank robbery, an incident occurred at the State House in Boston which reopened the wounds festering on Nantucket. In the midst of a listless session in the House of Representatives, a member quietly arose and addressed the Chair:

"Mr. Speaker."

"For what purpose does the gentleman rise?"

"To offer a resolution, Mr. Speaker, that an additional Notary Public be appointed for Nantucket."

Micajah Coffin sat bolt upright. Had he heard this last resolution correctly? For fourteen years he had been Nantucket's sole representative in the House. Now, on this pleasant June day, a Boston member was suddenly intervening in a purely Nantucket matter. Micajah rose from his seat and demanded to know where the Boston member had acquired the information on which he based his resolution.

"From a respectable gentleman from Nantucket," replied the Honorable Benjamin Russell.

The resolve was adopted without further discussion and the Speaker moved on to other business. Perplexed by the proceedings, Micajah moodily slumped into his seat. Was something being sneaked past him? As the Quaker guardian of the affairs of Nantucket, he felt himself compelled to look further into the matter.

By this time Russell had left his seat and was talking with some friends in a little passageway off the Chamber, but still within the walls of the House. Micajah strode across the Chamber and, interrupting Russell, he curtly asked him to identify the respectable gentleman he had referred to on the House floor.

"Why," said Russell carelessly, "his name's Coffin. Of course, I know there's a lot of Coffins on Nantucket, and this one is probably a cousin of yours."

Russell then pointed out William Coffin on the Speaker's rostrum. William Coffin was a guest in the House for the day, and he was seated behind the Speaker's chair, waiting to be introduced. He was trying to get the Notary Public appointment for a Nantucket friend, and he had put his request in through a mainland representative to avoid his archenemy, Micajah Coffin. When Micajah saw Russell point out William Coffin, his face turned all colors of the rainbow.

"What, that convict?" he exploded.

"What on earth are you talking about?" asked Russell in surprise.

"Don't thee know the business of the Nantucket Bank?" retorted Micajah.

"Yes," replied Russell, "but he was honorably acquitted."

"That did not make him the less guilty, thee knows," said Micajah in a loud voice as he turned on his heel and stomped away angrily.

A small crowd of members had collected in the passageway, and Micajah's vehement words were clearly heard by all those present. When these words were repeated to William Coffin a few minutes later, his face also became purple with rage but he kept control of himself and said nothing.

Micajah Coffin, the most zealous member of the Quaker prosecution at the time of the bank robbery, was a distant cousin of William Coffin. They were separated by four generations, and Micajah looked down on the younger man as a poor relation. William Coffin thought Micajah a bully, a bigot, and a pious fraud. Now these two antagonists squared off for the final battle.

William waited to make his move until both he and Micajah were back on Nantucket, a couple of weeks after the incident in the House. He confronted Micajah deliberately in the Nantucket Marine Insurance Company office.

"Will you apologize for your slanderous remarks in the House?" he asked.

"No. A thousand times no," Micajah replied obstinately.

"Why, you old rascal!" cried William seizing the dignified Micajah's nose in his huge hand and wringing it until the blood began to spurt.

As a result of this assault, William was attacked from all directions. The insurance company demanded that he apologize for insulting its office with violence. Micajah sued him for assault and battery. Micajah's sons stopped him on the street and menacingly demanded to know why he had laid violent hands on their father.

"Because he insulted me in such a manner that I could not get at him in the law," was William's honest answer. It was true. Under the State Constitution, legislative debates were privileged, and members could not be sued for slander for their remarks in the House.[2]

Micajah marched ahead with his assault-and-battery action. William fought the case all the way to the Supreme Judicial Court but ultimately lost it and had to pay Micajah fifteen dollars for tweaking his nose.[3] Micajah thus regained some of his lost dignity, but William was determined to have revenge. Despite Micajah's strong defense of constitutional privilege, William instituted an action for slander. A Nantucket jury awarded him fifteen dollars for the slanderous remarks uttered in the House and put him even with Micajah. This satisfied neither of the scrapping Coffins, and they both appealed. The case was retried before a Boston jury.

In the second jury trial, the judge instructed the jury that, if they found that Micajah had slandered William, then William should not be "turned off with such slight damages to make it better to seek personal revenge than to resort to the Law of the Country."

This instruction must have done it, for the Boston jury, unaware that William had already taken his "personal revenge" on Micajah, returned a verdict for $2,500 in his favor. Still hoping that his constitutional privilege would save him, Micajah appealed the case to the Supreme Judicial Court. There wasn't much doubt that Micajah's remarks in the House were slanderous, and he never denied that he had made them. The legal issue was whether or not they were privileged.

[2] Article 21 of the Declaration of Rights of the Massachusetts Constitution reads in part as follows: "The freedom of deliberation, speech and debate in either house of the legislature is so essential to the rights of the people, that it cannot be the foundation of any accusation or prosecution, action or complaint in any other Court or place whatsoever."

[3] *Coffin* v. *Coffin*, 2 Mass. 358 (1807).

On March 1, 1808, the eve of the appeal hearing, the influential Micajah pushed a resolve through the House that "words spoken by any member within the walls of the House . . . are alone and exclusively cognizable by this House. . . ."[4] This put the Supreme Judicial Court in a dilemma. Did the Constitution allow the courts to find Micajah guilty of slander, or was this a matter for the legislature to decide?

In a forty-four-page opinion, the court found that Micajah and his friends in the House could not enlarge their constitutional privilege against slander suits by a legislative resolve. The court then upheld the lawmakers' privilege in the abstract, but held it didn't apply to Micajah. True, he had uttered the fatal words within the walls of the House, but the Speaker had passed onto other business by the time he got around to uttering them. Thus, Micajah was not advancing the business of the House when he spoke out, and his slanderous words were not privileged. Micajah would have to pay William the $2,500.

The court concluded with the following bit of unsolicited advice in an effort to quell the Coffin vendetta. "It is not the province of the Court to advise either party, but as the jury have done ample justice to the plaintiff's character, we are satisfied that a liberal remission of a part of the damages could not in any manner operate to the plaintiff's dishonor. . . ."[5]

William paid no attention to these words of wisdom from the Supreme Judicial Court. The minute he laid hands on the execution in the late spring of 1808, he directed the sheriff to seize

[4] Chapter 1, Section 3, Article 10 of the Massachusetts Constitution empowers the House of Representatives "to settle the rules and orders of proceedings in their own House."

Here is the text of Micajah's resolve which he hoped would void the $2,500 jury verdict.

> Resolved: That words spoken by any member within the walls, relative to a subject under their consideration either in their separate capacity or in a convention of both branches of the Legislature; (whether the member speaking such words, addresses himself, in debate to the chair, or deliberates and advises with another member respecting the subject) are alone and exclusively cognizable by this house: and that for any tribunal or department of government to interfere with its authority and take cognizance of words thus spoken is a breach of the rights and privileges of this house, and a flagrant violation of that important article of the Constitution which expressly provides for "the freedom of deliberation, speech and debate in each house of the legislature."

[5] *Coffin v. Coffin*, 4 Mass. 2, 45 (1808).

Micajah's house, garden, sheep commons, and other property on Nantucket to satisfy the $2,500 jury verdict. Micajah didn't have the cash to satisfy this verdict, and his sons had to put up the cash before William would permit the return of the property. William went even farther than this. He pointedly threatened to sue any other "veterans in mischief and calumny" who dared to slander him in the future.

Both the combatants in this legal battle continued on as popular and highly successful men. The self-righteous Micajah was repeatedly reelected to the legislature until he retired at the age of eighty, at which time the grateful town elected his eldest son to serve in his stead. Micajah continued to believe that William Coffin masterminded the bank robbery. William Coffin, who became a prominent humanitarian on the Island, continued to regard Micajah as a mischief maker and a humbug. Neither man would deign to talk to the other the rest of their lives, and they remained mortal enemies to the grave.

8
Law of the Sea

"By God, she's a full-rigged ship with two of her masts gone over the side," muttered the South Tower watchman as his spyglass swept the shoals northwest of Muskegat Island. From his vantage point, atop the Town's highest building, he was able to look over the flat island and see the vast expanse of ocean on all sides. The northwest gale shook the tower to its foundations and made it difficult to train the spyglass on the distant horizon. "Still too gray to be sure," thought the watchman resting his eye; but when the red rim of the sun rose behind him in the east, his final doubts dissolved. "She's stuck fast, all right—must be distress signals flying from the mainmast," he concluded as he bounded down the tower stairs. Although the sun was barely up, his news traveled fast. Within minutes the Town knew another wreck was taking place.

The full-rigged ship *British Queen*, carrying Irish immigrants from Dublin to New York, had struck the shoals on the Nantucket side of Muskegat Channel during the night in a blinding snowstorm. Now, as December 18, 1851, dawned clear and cold, the continuing northwest gale piled up angry-looking whitecaps all around her. Winter had arrived early on Nantucket that year. In addition to the freezing spray which clogged the rigging of the boats in the harbor, huge ice floes blocked the harbor's entrance and filled Nantucket Sound. The early freeze cut off communication with the mainland. The watchful islanders knew that, under these conditions, there was no way of reaching the wreck, which lay several miles offshore, until the gale abated.

Although the *British Queen* had managed to fly distress signals from her one remaining mast, the islanders had no way of knowing who was aboard or what cargo she carried. At that time wireless had not yet been invented, and signal flags were the only way of communicating at sea. However, these all important signal flags had a limited usefulness. They could only be read during the daylight hours, and, even with good visibility, they were difficult to read.

The islanders were accustomed to wrecks. Before the Cape Cod Canal was built in 1914, Nantucket Sound was the main shipping lane along the coast. By the mid-nineteenth century, 18,000 vessels passed through the Sound annually and only a few hundred of these were steamers; the rest were clumsy sailing vessels which often had to beat against the wind. In the era of scanty navigational aids, the rips and shoals around Nantucket claimed a record number of wrecks.

Since the days of Tristram Coffin, the islanders had supplemented their meager livelihoods by salvaging wrecks. By the mid-nineteenth century salvage operations had become professionalized and the competition between rival Island wreckers was keen and sometimes bitter. Usually the first person or persons to reach a wreck reaped the largest rewards, although, under Admiralty law, the first salvor on the spot did not necessarily have an absolute right to perform the entire rescue.[1] Most of the wrecks around Nantucket were sloops, schooners and brigs; the wreck of a bark or a large, full-rigged ship was a rarity which inflamed the imaginations of the wreckers and emboldened them to perform extreme acts of daring.

In 1851 the steamboat line which ran between Nantucket and the mainland maintained two boats, the *Massachusetts* and the *Telegraph*. During the December freeze, the *Telegraph* happened to be icebound at Nantucket. These steamboats often took part in salvage operations on a professional basis.[2] At this time,

[1] *The Amethyst*, D.C.Me. 1840, 1 Fed.Case 762 No. 330, 2 Ware 28.
[2] A few years after this happened, the insurer of the steamboat line excluded professional salvage from its insurance contract because of the dangerous nature of the work and the steamboats ceased to perform salvage as a sideline to their passenger- and cargo-carrying activities.

when the wrecking business on Nantucket was at its peak, the steamboat company employed a resident wreckmaster named Thomas Gardner.

When Thomas Gardner heard of the wreck, he immediately engaged Captain William Patterson and his schooner, *Gamecock*, to assist the *Telegraph* in a joint salvage operation. Gardner's plan was to have the *Telegraph* tow the schooner *Gamecock* through the ice fields to the wreck; it was too dangerous for the *Telegraph* to go it alone. If the steamboat's paddles became disabled in the ice, she was very likely to end up a wreck herself.

Captain William Patterson's brother, Captain David Patterson, was part owner of the *Hamilton*, another small schooner also used for salvage operations. The wrecking crews of the *Hamilton* and the *Gamecock* were bitter rivals. David Patterson was an outstanding seaman who had recently taken a fifty-foot schooner around the Horn to California. When he learned of the wreck, he decided to hazard the *Hamilton* on a salvage attempt and he immediately contacted Peter Folger, the resident underwriters' agent on Nantucket. As agent for the Marine Insurance Companies, Folger was authorized to hire wreckers to salvage ships' cargoes.

"Frankly, I don't think it's worth a try," said Peter Folger to David Patterson as the two men helped themselves to an early morning mug up before the pot-bellied stove of a snug little office down by the waterfront. "Gardner has the *Telegraph* right here in the harbor, and he's probably already engaged your brother Bill's schooner. Now where does that leave you?"

"Peter, nobody's going anywhere in this gale today," replied David Patterson. "Now, you just engage the *Hamilton* on behalf of the underwriters, and I'll make sure it's all right with my partner, Macy. That ship's hard aground and she'll have to accept all the help she can get."[3]

"You know I'll engage you, David—I always do—but how will you ever get out of the harbor and through the ice without the *Telegraph* to tow you over the bar?" asked Folger.

"First, I'll pass the word to my man, Captain Bearse, to get

---

[3] There is no legal duty to accept an offer of help and the vessel in trouble can pick whichever salvor she wants. "A vessel in distress is not to be killed by kindness. . . ." *The Moser,* 55 F 2d 904.

the *Hamilton* ready. Then, I'll drop out of sight and get a little shut-eye until the gale moderates. Gardner and my brother Bill will never suspect I'm having anything to do with this. Here's what we do . . ." said Patterson as Folger shook his head in disbelief.

All day long the northwest gale shrieked over Nantucket, as the islanders waited for the wreck to break up. Some small boats from Tuckernuck Island tried to get out to her, but they were blown back without getting close. At nightfall, the watchman in the Tower reported that the wreck was still intact although the gale continued to blow hard.

On the following morning, the *Telegraph* got up steam at 5:30 in the inky darkness. A little while later, there was a bustle of activity on the *Gamecock*, but the *Hamilton* remained lifeless. Thomas Gardner began to feel he had stolen a march on his rival, David Patterson.

The gale continued to blow out of the north, straight into the harbor's mouth. This made it impossible for the *Telegraph* to tow the *Gamecock* across the sandbar which lay across the harbor's entrance until high tide at 1:00 P.M. Even at high tide there would be only nine feet of water covering the bar. The *Gamecock* drew seven.

The rival schooners, *Gamecock* and *Hamilton*, remained tied up at Straight Wharf all morning. On the stroke of noon, the *Telegraph* towed the *Gamecock* around Brant Point and headed for the bar. Just as they were leaving, David Patterson sauntered down onto the wharf and waved them a cheery good-bye.

The *Telegraph*, with the *Gamecock* in tow, made it over the bar and through the ice to the site of the wreck, about nine miles distant from the harbor entrance. The *Telegraph* managed to anchor about three-quarters of a mile from the wreck, while the *Gamecock*, with wreckmaster Gardner aboard, edged in as close to the wreck as she could get.

Gardner was elated. Everything was going according to plan. He had managed to get both vessels safely through the ice and there, only a few yards in front of him, lay the large ship waiting to be salvaged. "By God, I've got him this time!" he exclaimed to Captain Bill Patterson as he thought of David Patterson stranded back at Straight Wharf.

Half an hour after the *Telegraph* had towed the *Gamecock* around Brant Point, the *Hamilton* had gotten under way with pilot David Patterson on board. The *Hamilton* drew eight feet of water, a foot more than the *Gamecock*, and her rivals never dreamt she would be able to beat over the bar under sail and plow through the ice to the wreck. But that is what she did. When she arrived at the wreck site, she sent a small boat over to the *Telegraph* with David Patterson aboard. They picked up Gardner's assistant, Captain Russell, and proceeded in the small boat out to the *Gamecock*.

Gardner was so preoccupied overseeing the salvage operation that he never noticed the arrival of the *Hamilton*.

"Whose boat is that?" yelled Gardner as the small rowboat came alongside.

"David Patterson's," came back the answer.

"Why, I left him at the wharf," exploded Gardner.

"Well, he's here now," piped up Russell, "and you'd better invite him to join us."

Grudgingly, Gardner jumped into the small boat and seized the steering oar. "Pull," he commanded and the boat headed for the wreck. About halfway to the wreck, some low breakers suddenly showed their white teeth. "Captain Patterson, you'd better take the steering oar," said Gardner. "You are more acquainted with these breakers than I."

Grabbing the oar, Patterson took the boat safely through the breakers. The wreck lay with her stern to the tide and the *Gamecock* had been drifted down to within fifty feet of her. Still there was room for the rowboat to pass down between the two vessels. Patterson noticed that the current was rapidly sweeping them down the wreck's side.

"Steady!" he yelled as he spotted a ladder hanging over the side. With a single sweep of the steering oar, he swung the rowboat around so that her stern fetched up at the ladder. "Get her away," he bellowed as he scrambled up the ladder. The men at the oars pulled for their lives as the little boat, swept down by the current, shot past the wreck's bow.

Patterson clawed his way aft, along the wreck's icy, canted decks, in search of the ship's captain. The wreck was half-sunk and about to break up at any moment. There was no time to lose.

"I don't have any cargo and she's not insured, but please save as many of my passengers as you can," pleaded Captain Conway.

By this time Gardner had been able to board and he quickly hoisted a signal for the *Gamecock* to lay alongside. The *Gamecock* was drifted down by the wreck, but she couldn't be held there because of the surge. One minute she was under the wreck's counter; the next, she was riding high above her rail.

"How many passengers have you got, Captain?" asked Patterson.

"Two hundred twenty-four, not counting the two who died last night," replied Conway.

Patterson and Gardner looked at each other inquiringly. How many passengers could be saved before the tide turned west at 4:00 P.M. and brought the huge swells left over from the gale crashing along the wreck's starboard side? Gardner's Adam's apple began to work up and down. "I'll do my best," he promised.

The passengers began to jump aboard the *Gamecock*, but it was slow work. Many of them were half-frozen and could hardly move.

"We're setting down on the shoal," reported the *Gamecock*. "No more, please—we'll be lucky to get off as it is."

It was obvious to those in charge that, before the *Gamecock* could transfer the passengers to the *Telegraph* and return for a second trip, the tide would turn and make a second trip impossible. The *Gamecock* had managed to take off only sixty passengers.

Stepping forward and drawing some code flags from his pocket, Patterson spoke to Captain Conway. "We get nothing for saving lives but, be assured, my schooner will save your people. I only hope Captain Gardner will agree to share whatever salvage is collected with me for my crew."[4]

Gardner stared hard at David Patterson for one long moment. Then he rushed toward him and shook his hand. A moment later Gardner was gone. "Good luck!" he yelled over his shoulder

[4] It was odd but true. Under Admiralty law there is no reward for saving lives unless the ship or its cargo are also saved. *The Zephyrus* 1842, 1 W.Rob. 329.

as he jumped from the wreck's rail onto the deck of the departing *Gamecock*.

Patterson hoisted his private signal flags on the wreck's mainmast. Captain Bearse, aboard the *Hamilton*, carefully paid out his anchor line to lay along the wreck's starboard side, which was low in the water and nearest the shoal. The tide was still running east, but the breakers were kicking up worse than ever, smashing over the wreck's stern and covering the decks with freezing spray.

"Let's get going!" snapped Patterson as he started throwing passengers onto the *Hamilton*'s deck. The *Hamilton* began to set down on the shoal with jarring smashes as the passengers were being tossed aboard.

"No, we don't quit till everyone's off," Patterson repeated again and again. At last he hollered to Bearse, "That's it." Bearse gave the order to kedge the *Hamilton* off the shoal as Patterson jumped aboard. The *Hamilton* was now so heavily laden that it seemed she would never get off. Then, suddenly, they found themselves in deep water, and Captain Bearse ran up the jib.

"For the love of Christmas, will you look at that!" Patterson shouted to Bearse. Just as the *Hamilton* was getting under way, a small fishing smack, with three men aboard, anchored in the channel and two of her crew rowed to the wreck. Carelessly tying their skiff to the wreck's bobstay, they proceeded to scoop up small bits of her running rigging. Legally, they had a right to do this.[5] What attracted Patterson's attention was not their salvage attempts, but the fact that they appeared determined to stay on the wreck until dark.

"Get off, you damned fools!" shouted Bearse. But the two fishermen merely waved back.

Patterson consulted his pocket watch. "In five minutes the tide goes west—then God help them," he proclaimed. "We have enough problems of our own getting all these passengers in before dark."

The *Hamilton* headed for the harbor, and the long Decem-

[5] A voluntary salvor not only has a right to strip an abandoned wreck, but the maritime law gives him a possessory lien to hold onto the equipment taken. See *The Snow Maiden* 1957, American Maritime Cases, 2093, a case in which one of the authors represented the salvor.

ber night began to close in. As she disappeared, the tide turned west. The two fishermen crawled into their skiff, which was loaded with the wreck's rigging, just as a huge swell broke over the wreck smashing the skiff against her side. The skiff was half-swamped, and the fishermen were thrown into the sea.

The *Hamilton* discharged her passengers at Straight Wharf shortly after 5:00 P.M. Not a single passenger had been lost, except for the two who had died aboard the ship the night before. The survivors, however, had a sad tale to tell.

The *British Queen* was a large ship but a very old one. The ships which brought Irish immigrants to our shores in the wake of the Irish potato famine were usually operated on a shoestring and were called "coffin ships" because of their unseaworthiness. The *British Queen* was no exception.

Her trip across the Atlantic, in the teeth of westerly gales, had taken eight weeks. In the course of this extra-long voyage, fever had broken out among the passengers. Captain Conway was sick himself, unable to stand long watches on deck. As the ship approached our shores, foul weather prevented the ship's officers from taking celestial observations, and she strayed off course. At last she sighted Nantucket's south shore, but this was not where she was supposed to be. By this time she was already in the tricky shoal-strewn passage between Nantucket and Martha's Vineyard known as Muskegat Channel. The northwest gale forced her to tack back and forth across the channel, and the early snowstorm made it impossible to see anything forward of the mast.

The big ship took in sail and started to take short hitches north and west. While beating in a northerly direction, she overstood and went hard on the shoal on the starboard side of the channel. She hit so hard that her foremast snapped at the deck and went over the side in the darkness. The lurching of the ship snapped the mizzenmast at midnight. Captain Conway had the tangled rigging cut away in an attempt to lighten the ship and keep her afloat. For forty hours the passengers clung to life in the freezing, water-filled hold, expecting every minute to be their last.

When the *Hamilton* arrived at Straight Wharf with the last load of passengers, the townspeople were waiting for her in the cold darkness. They led the suffering passengers away to their homes and various public halls. Many of the immigrants were cared for in a public hall which is now the site of the Island's Catholic Church. The Nantucketers were generous in their gifts of food and clothing which were rare commodities on the Island in wintertime. Because of the ship's fever, the immigrants' clothing was burned immediately and they were given new clothes. Thus, the immigrants arrived in America without even the shirts on their backs. "May God Almighty bless you," they repeated again and again to their Island hosts in the course of the evening.

David Patterson crouched over the *Hamilton's* bilge with a lantern in his hand and muttered to himself. "Something must have sprung with all that pounding, but she seems to be all right."

"Captain Patterson," someone shouted into the hold. "One of the fishermen we left at the wreck just sailed in. He says the other two are still trapped out there on the ice."

"Here we go again," thought Patterson. "Guess I'll have to make a second trip up to see Macy."

"Don't let the safety of the vessel enter into the matter in the least," replied merchant Joseph B. Macy, when he was asked to let the *Hamilton* attempt a second rescue. "But take care of yourself, David," he said "The Island needs you."

The following day, the islanders scanned the ice floes for the missing fishermen. It was impossible to tell whether the specks they saw on the ice were bits of wreckage or men. Just as evening fell once more, the *Hamilton* passed over the bar. Her starboard anchor was catted, all set to let go as she crept along the edge of the ice. Patterson's plan was to have a shore party light a range light as soon as the fishermen were spotted and have the *Hamilton* sail directly for the light.

"There goes the light," the lookout reported.

"Keep swinging that lead," yelled the helmsman as the *Hamilton* headed inshore. Her disappointed crew soon discovered a large piece of wreckage in the ice, which the shore party had mistaken for the fishermen. After two more hours of constant soundings and fruitless searching, the *Hamilton's* men began to get discouraged. Patterson quickly devised a final, desperate plan which he revealed to Bearse.

"Run down that jib and head her for the beach," Bearse ordered. All sail was taken in and the *Hamilton,* under bare poles, was kept directly before the wind. Soon she was jammed in the thick ice, sideways to the beach.

"Captain Allen, you stay here with two men," said Patterson jumping onto the ice. "The rest of you, follow me." By this time the moon was up and the search party spread out on the ice floes and started to march south. About a mile south from the schooner, the fishermen's boat was finally spotted about a quarter of a mile from the shore. The search party was relieved to see two heads appear above the gunwale. The boat, however, was surrounded by thin ice and water and could not be reached by foot.

"You stay here and keep them awake," Patterson told one of the crew. "The rest of us will go after a skiff and an ox team." Before the search party returned, the two fishermen managed to crawl ashore on two narrow strips of board which they tore out of the rise of their boat. They were picked up on the beach more dead than alive, but they recovered within a few weeks.

Now came the job of making sure the *Hamilton* wasn't lost in the ice. She was slowly and laboriously kedged out to the edge of the ice pack and then sailed triumphantly back into the harbor.

As far as David Patterson was concerned, it was all part of his day's work. Over the next fifteen years, he compiled a sensational record as a pilot and a wrecker. Sometimes he would refloat wrecks and pilot them all the way to New York. At other times he would rig breeches buoys of his own design and would be the first one whisked aboard inshore wrecks. Patterson often employed crews of thirty or more wreckers. On one occasion he was presented with a silver watch by the King of Prussia for saving a German ship. Despite his many heroic feats, Patterson did not make a great fortune as a wrecker. He simply knew his business and enjoyed doing it well.

On Christmas Day 1851, the survivors of the *British Queen* were taken to the mainland on the *Telegraph* and eventually made their way to New York. One young couple, however, who had just been married in Dublin at the start of the voyage, remained behind. After eight weeks at sea and two nights of terror, the Robert Mooneys vowed "never again" as they stepped onto Straight Wharf. True to their word, neither of them ever left Nantucket again. The only possession they managed to bring ashore was a family crucifix. Robert Mooney settled down on the Island as a tenant farmer, and with his wife raised a family of seven children. Nantucket was the only part of America they ever saw.

The *British Queen* broke up soon after the rescue and was sold as she lay for $290. Little of her equipment was salvaged. A few days after she disappeared, the ship's quarterboard bearing the words "British Queen" carved in wood was found on the beach wrapped in seaweed. It was presented to Robert Mooney, who proudly hung it on the barn of the Mooney farm on Polpis Road, where it became a familiar landmark.

Today this quarterboard hangs over the present Robert Mooney's fireplace. On stormy nights, when the waves are crashing on the beach, we often gaze at this last remnant of the *British Queen* and wonder at the trials and tribulations of our great-grandparents as we drink a toast to Captain Patterson and the other Island wreckers whose heroic efforts made this our Island home.

9

The Ghost of Tristram Coffin

"How's the campaign coming along, Squire?" asked a curious dockside worker.

"Coming along just fine," answered a slim man in a black frockcoat as he shot past the docks and turned up Main Street. Anyone could tell from the light blue eyes and finely chiseled features under the top hat that he was a Coffin, and everyone on Nantucket knew that, in this crucial election year of 1880, this particular Coffin was running for Governor.

"Why, that's his second trip to the Post Office today. Wonder what he's up to," said a shopkeeper on Main Street. The candidate, who was carrying two very large bundles of letters, suddenly broke into a trot and disappeared inside the building.

As the Island's only lawyer, Allen Coffin was always on the run. In order to stay afloat on Nantucket, he was forced to combine politics, law, and business in his activities. Unknown to most islanders, however, his present burst of energy had nothing to do with running for Governor. The new project which he was so feverishly launching soon proved to be the most imaginative scheme ever carried out on the Island.

Nantucket had reached the zenith of her prosperity some forty years before, in the early 1840s. At that time she had a whaling fleet of ninety ships, a population verging on 10,000 and a sheep herd of 20,000. Then the blows to her prosperity fell in quick succession.

Nantucket had never had a serious fire. From the seventeenth century up until 1832, the total fire loss is estimated to have been less than $36,000, brought about mainly by the destruction of isolated houses. Then, in July 1846, tragedy overtook the Island as three hundred wooden buildings, covering thirty-three acres in the center of Town, went up in smoke. Barrel upon barrel of whale oil caught fire and were destroyed. The property damage ran to over a million dollars. The whaling industry's equipment, ropewalks, sail lofts, and boatyards were completely destroyed, and many Nantucketers were left penniless.

Following this disaster, shifting sands blocked the harbor's entrance so that the large, heavily ladened, whalers could not enter. The discovery of oil in Pennsylvania and the California Gold Rush of 1849 hastened the industry's decline. During the Civil War, Confederate raiders picked off the last of the slow-sailing whaling ships. In 1869 the last whaling ship sailed from Nantucket, never to return. The sheep industry had died during the sheep wars of the 1850s, and now the whaling industry was also dead.

In 1870 Nantucket hit bottom economically. The population had declined from a high of 12,000 to under 3,000. Codfishing was again tried in the village of 'Sconset on the outer side of the Island, but it never became a financial success. Impoverished families fled to the mainland, and their furniture was thrown out in the streets to be auctioned off or burned. There was a feeling of utter hopelessness in the air. Nantucketers simply melted away, too dispirited even to leave forwarding addresses. These later migrations were a more serious drain on the population than the earlier ones had been because, now that the whaling industry had turned belly-up, the dispersed whalers would never return to the Island.

In despair, the few families that remained started taking in summer boarders, and it was in this fashion that Nantucket's summer-resort industry was slowly kindled. A visit by President Grant in 1874 added impetus to the resort business, and Grant was followed by a series of Presidents, ex-Presidents and other dignitaries who began to learn of the charms of old Nantucket.

During the pre-Civil War period of Nantucket's prosperity, Zenas Coffin had become the Island's wealthiest shipowner. He built many graceful mansions for the members of his family in the Town and, among his many widespread holdings, he retained a goodly share of the sheep commons. Zenas was too busy making money at sea to keep track of his complex interests in the sheep pastures which yielded no income; however, he wasn't afraid of losing his rights in them. He knew that if a small landowner tried to establish title, some Coffin partial interest was bound to surface, at which point he would have ample opportunity to assert his rights. During this period of economic boom, other large landowners followed his example and behaved like sleepy cats keeping an eye on mice.

Following the Civil War, the sons of Zenas Coffin, Charles and Henry Coffin, were forced by economic circumstances to turn their backs on the sea and try to develop the land lying outside the Town, left empty by the decline of the sheep industry. In a period of twenty years, the two Coffin brothers completed 400 land transactions on the Island.

Their first major attempt at land development was the Cliff on the Island's north shore. In 1872 they paid in sheep commons to the Proprietorship and had this area set off to them in individual ownership. They then subdivided the land into house lots for vacation homes. Although they managed to sell one large lot to New York's leading trial lawyer, Charles O'Conor, for a retirement home, the scheme was a financial bust because Nantucket wasn't yet ready for land development.

In 1880, undismayed by this failure, the Coffin brothers turned their attention to Surfside, which is located on the Island's south shore. It soon became clear that this second real estate development attempt was likely to be an even bigger financial failure than the first unless something was done to draw buyers to Nantucket.

At this time the prospects of the Island's economic survival were a bit brighter. The federal government, after years of petitioning by the islanders, had started construction of two parallel jetties in front of the harbor's mouth to prevent the channel from filling in with sand. Winter scalloping was initiated, and the delicious little Island scallops provided the islanders with some income during the months when there were no tourists. Finally, a group of mainland financiers proposed the construction of a railroad on the Island.

The Coffin brothers arranged to have this tiny railroad run from the Town docks, where the steamboats arrived, to their new development on the south shore at Surfside. Later a branch was extended to 'Sconset. The railroad ran until World War I, when its tracks were torn up and shipped to the mainland for use in the war effort.

Once a distraught western railroad wired the stationmaster in search of some missing boxcars which had wandered off its line. "Could they be in Nantucket?" came the inquiry.

"Not unless they have fins," wired back the stationmaster.

These developments were promising, but an additional ingredient was desperately needed to restore the Island's prosperity. At this point Allen Coffin unveiled his fantastic scheme. Tristram Coffin had died almost 200 years before, in 1681. Why not hold a family reunion on Nantucket in 1881 to lure back all those thousands of living descendants from around the world? Tristram's heirs were now so numerous that any significant gathering of the clan was bound to create prosperity for the Coffins still living on the Island.

Feverishly, Squire Coffin set to work mailing out letters to off-island Coffins and the enthusiastic response indicated that the proposed reunion would be an outstanding success. By the beginning of 1881, Squire Coffin's unsuccessful campaign for Governor was behind him, and his new plan for economic survival was running along in high gear. He had prepared every imaginable kind of souvenir for the upcoming reunion, including medals, plates, and replicas of the supposed Coffin coat of arms. He was hard at work writing a history of Tristram Coffin, which he felt was bound to be a best seller among the Coffin clan and would offset the costs of the entire promotion. He even proposed erecting some sort of memorial statue of Tristram on the Island, figuring that although it would cause further expense it would provide a tangible rallying point for the reunion.

The landowning Coffin brothers, who were busy seeing to

the completion of the railroad so it would be operating in time for the reunion, optimistically divided their Surfside land into smaller and smaller lots. Surely the off-island Coffins would want to own summer cottages near the grave of their famous ancestor. Then, suddenly, an unexpected calamity clouded the financial outlook of the entire project.

Fifty Coffin descendants had arrived on Nantucket to plan the upcoming gathering. Squire Coffin ran the meeting. Everything was going according to plan when a female Coffin descendant rose from her seat. She was a forerunner of the Feminist Movement who was a fully ordained minister in the Universalist Church, and she proposed a bronze statue to honor Dionis as well as Tristram. Immediately, another lady jumped to her feet and seconded the motion for "a bronze statue of husband and wife on one pedestal side by side."[1]

It was true that Dionis had been the faithful wife who had poured the beer in Newbury which had helped pay for Nantucket. It was also true that she had stood up to the Magistrates and had been acquitted of overcharging for her beer. But Squire Coffin, in his wildest imagination, had never dreamed that this bit of history would require an enormous bronze statue. Here was the best money-making project of his entire career being deflected into a grandiose scheme which was likely to create a ruinous debt.

Now that the ladies had gotten up steam, their fervor knew no bounds. A lady sculptor was contacted and came up with an estimate for the proposed statue of $10,000. Squire Coffin was in despair. A lady, using the nom de plume of "Jetty," wrote to the newspaper:

> The statue of Dionis should be placed where there will be an opportunity of placing that of her husband not far away.
>
> I would have her standing on the outer end of the jetty: She should be dressed in the simple garb of the

[1] Bronze statues became enormously popular in America during the years following the Civil War. (See Chapter 17, about the statue of General Hooker on his war-horse.) They have remained an important part of the Massachusetts political scene up until recent times. (See Chapter 3, about the statue of Mary Dyer.)

Society of Friends. I would have her standing in a determined, confident position. In one hand she should hold a torch raised aloft which at all times would be useful as a beacon, and with her other hand she should be holding to her lips a long trumpet. This trumpet should be connected by pipes with the shore and blown in foggy weather—thus the statue could be seen and heard.

"Jetty" then went on to describe how Tristram's statue should be perched on the opposite jetty, then under federal construction, and closed with the following suggestion: "His face should be beaming with calm delight as he gazes out at his brave wife and welcomes those who approach our shores."

The reunion took place during three days in August. Five hundred Coffins descended on Nantucket. The railroad's locomotive had been named Dionis, and she had to make two trips to haul all the Coffins out to Surfside. The railroad terminal shed at Surfside was used for the reunion headquarters so that the off-island Coffins would be fully exposed to the charms of the nearby Coffin building lots.

As the assembled Coffin clan listened in awed silence, Miss Mary Coffin Johnson, who had just returned from England, described the Coffin ancestral manor in Devonshire:

A full half mile on a winding road overshadowed by noble oaks and the ancient homestead is reached. J.R. Pine-Coffin, lord of Portledge Manor, receives you and leads you into the square and stately hall with an arched ceiling. Around the hall at the upper story is a balustrade forming a gallery, upon the walls of which hang the family portraits of the ancestral Coffins, men and women of past generations and centuries.

Mary Coffin Johnson had done some further research and had traced the Coffin name all the way back to its French origin in Normandy, but it was Portledge Manor which captured the imagination of the reunion. Portledge Manor had been in the Coffin family for over 800 years. As there were numerous Coffins in southwest England, however, it was unclear just what Tristram's connection had been with the manor, or if there had been any connection at all. Despite the lack of historical basis, Squire Coffin had prepared numerous pictures of Portledge Manor, and they were soon sold out.

Judge Owen Tristram Coffin of Poughkeepsie, New York, was the reunion's keynote speaker. He was a gifted orator and historian. Carried away with emotion, he purchased the old Jethro Coffin House during the reunion and donated it as a memorial to the Coffin family.

Judge Coffin was a descendant of the devout Quaker Abishai Coffin, who fled up the Hudson River at the time of the Revolution and now had over 400 descendants living in the Hudson River Valley. He described the glories of the Coffin family in America, and his speech was met with deafening applause. Other speeches followed, interspersed with patriotic renderings by a brass band. A crowded schedule of clambakes, fishing parties, and dances kept the clan busy for the remainder of the reunion.

At the end of an enjoyable three days, the off-island Coffins packed up and departed. A determined effort to trace Tristram's ancestry back to William the Conqueror had failed. No one could decide on a proper site for the bronze statue, and only $200 had been subscribed to cover its $10,000 estimated cost. Furthermore, it came to light that none of the Nantucket Coffins had subscribed a single penny. The only explanation that Squire Coffin could give was that the Nantucket Coffins were just waiting to see what the statue would look like.

The most sobering fact was that few of the Coffin brothers' Surfside lots had been sold. Eventually, the Surfside development had to be auctioned off, and then it went through bankruptcy. Squire Coffin kept himself busy during the 1890s representing the creditors.

Everyone who tried to develop the common lands outside the Town went broke. Without the sheep, the land appeared to be worthless. The miles of rolling moors remained unoccupied as Nantucket marched through two World Wars. The ghost of Tristram Coffin remained free to stalk the heather undisturbed.

10

Tales and Wails of the Litigants

The name of sturdy Stephen Hussey became synonymous with legal entanglements on Nantucket. A man of considerable property, born in Lynn, Massachusetts, he arrived carrying the first set of law books to the Island. Quickly shattering the harmonious plans of the first settlers, he became the first of Nantucket's notorious litigants. Armed with his weighty tomes, Hussey set about to involve himself in almost every controversy in Town. His name appears as plaintiff, defendant, or counsel in almost every court session of his day. His contentiousness gained him much enmity in the Town and his dealings with the Island Indians also became legendary. In 1687 he managed to obtain an Indian deed to 1,560 acres of valuable land in Pocomo. A few years later he was convicted of smuggling rum to the same Indians. In the years between he appeared as the advocate of the Indians in their petition addressed to Governor Joseph Dudley and the General Court to recover their land, drafting the following colorful language:

> Your petitioner's earnest prayer is that your Honors will allow him ye favor of a speciall Court to begin or bring his first action or order yt he may proceed or

bring such action at ye Inferior Court att Boston or at
any Court in Plymouth Colony as in your wisdom shall
be thought consistent, for yr petitioner dreads a tryall
upon Nantucket . . .

Hussey spent the remainder of his long life complaining that
he could never get a fair trial on Nantucket, while he continued
to wage his legal wars against his neighbors. Ever loyal to his life
at the law, he drafted his own will in 1718, and wrote: "To avoid
contests and janglings, I have made many wills heretofore, which
I now declare null and void, and this is my last will." After mentioning his wife and children, he ended it: "I give my Law Books
to my son Bachelor for the use of his son Stephen." And thus another Stephen Hussey was launched upon a legal career, while
the islanders shuddered at the prospect.

When Nantucket embarked upon its maritime adventures,
the importance of farming and sheep-raising diminished as the
islanders cast their eyes toward the sea. Thus, the Nantucketers
paid no heed to the impending problem which was closest to
them and soon to engulf them in floods of litigation: the ownership of the land of Nantucket. With the culmination of the great
Sheep Commons Fight which doomed the old Proprietorship in
1813, the major landowners obtained large parcels of the most
valuable farmland. The remaining land on the Island was generally considered to be of little value. Yet there still remained hundreds of acres owned by thousands of individuals. The titles became so fractionalized by inheritance that few could spend the
time or money required to clear their titles. As the economy of
the Island declined, the expense of litigation was simply not
worth the effort.

One of the memorable figures in Nantucket's land law in the
nineteenth century was neither lawyer nor litigant, but a shrewd
scholar and spectator of the local scene. As Register of Deeds, he
recorded much of the real estate lore with great wisdom and a
very colorful style. William Hussey Macy was born in Nantucket
in 1826, and went to sea on a whaler at age fifteen, making three
voyages before he enlisted in the Army during the Civil War. He
was wounded at the Battle of Kinston, North Carolina, serving
with General Burnside, and returned to Nantucket where he was

From *Automobile Quarterly*, Princeton Institute for Historic Research. (*Courtesy of Edouard A. Stackpole*).

Clinton S. Folger and his famous Overland, Nantucket's most notorious vehicle. (*Nantucket Historical Association*)

Clint Folger and his Horsemobile, delivering the mail to 'Sconset. (*Nantucket Historical Association*)

Frederick Douglass

Daniel Webster. (*Daguerreotype, 1850, in the Metropolitan Museum of Art, New York; gift of I. N. Phelps Stokes, Edward S. Hawes, Alice Mary Hawes, Marion Augusta Hawes, 1937*)

Codfish Park in the beginning. (*Nantucket Historical Association*)

W. F. Marshall, wrecked on Nantucket. (*Nantucket Historical Association*)

Old Town Building and Court House, Orange Street, Nantucket. (*Nantucket Historical Association*)

Hon. Reginald Taliaferro FitzRandolph, Justice of Nantucket District Court.

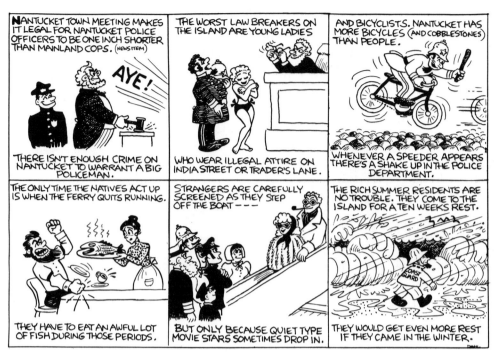

"The Law in Nantucket," by Francis Dahl, Boston *Herald*.

"There Will Always Be a Nantucket," by Francis Dahl, Boston *Herald*.

Steamer *Telegraph*. (*Courtesy of Charles F. Sayle*)

Ned Low, pirate. (*By permission of the Houghton Library, Harvard University; photo by Barry Donahue*)

The oldest house in Nantucket, Jethro Coffin House—1686. (*Nantucket Historical Association*)

Walter Folger, Jr., 1765–1848, legislator, judge, and genius. Artist unknown. (*Nantucket Historical Association*)

Admiral Sir Isaac Coffin, 1759–1839, Nantucket benefactor. (*Courtesy of The Coffin School*)

elected Register of Deeds in 1869. He served in the office until his death in 1891. In 1874 he lost his wife and was left with five young children to support and raise alone. The tragedy was increased when he went blind; in those days the Register was required to copy each deed into the official records by longhand. Fearing the possible legal complications to arise if the question of a blind man's fitness to hold the office should arise, Macy formally resigned, and one of his friends, Andrew Myrick, was elected. Yet Macy stayed in the office and continued to do the work, with the help of his hired assistant. For sixteen years he continued to draft and copy thousands of deeds and dictate hundreds of legal instruments. He also invented a machine of his own, which he called his "blind writer," and with it he turned out thousands of pages of readable manuscripts, including books and stories of the whaling days, newspaper and magazine articles. A collection of his works is preserved in the library of Perkins School for the Blind in Watertown, Massachusetts.

William H. Macy was considered the authority on the complications of Nantucket real estate titles, and wrote many descriptions of the sheep commons which are still valuable sources for understanding the Proprietorship and the land problems of the Island. As Register of Deeds, he was the one most frequently confronted with the old deeds and the old question: "I know I own it, but what is it?"

How much land do you own, Ma'am? Ah, well, that depends!
I was running over some old odds and ends,
And among them discovered this ragged old deed,
So discolored by time it is not easy to read.

It belonged to my father, long 'ere I was born,
He spent a large part of his life round Cape Horn.
And I don't think he knew what he owned when he died,
You'll find some more writing there on the back side.

Oh, yes, ma'am, tis duly recorded I see,
But don't you think he may have sold it? Not he!
If he owned any land he'd be quite sure to hold it,
So it isn't worth while to search whether he's sold it;

This deed gives him sheep commons ten and a quarter,
And, of course, what he owned all belongs to his daughter;
What I want to know now, is just what I own!
(She speaks with the air of a queen on her throne).
Of course I own land, there's writing to show it;
If it's worth any money then I want to know it!"

"Well, Madam, you'd better leave this for your heirs;
It's located in the Amendment Beach Shares;
Do you know where that is?" "No, indeed, I do not."
"Just two minutes walk brings you right to the spot;

If the tide's at the ebb and the time opportune,
'Tis down in the mud near the Bowling Saloon;
What your late father owned was one-seventieth part
Of a very small piece, as you will see by this chart;
And at present your land's not worth any bother,
Though it may be a bonanza some time or other;

The railroad may boom in some future day,
There have been stranger things." "But you don't mean to say
That they pasture their sheep down in mud holes like those."
"The sheep roamed at large and went there—if they chose.

Of course they'd find nothing but mud and salt water,
But 'tis there you own sheep commons—ten and a quarter."
"What's to pay?" in a tone of deep humiliation,
"We'll charge nothing, Madam, for this information."

—WILLIAM H. MACY

The advice of Macy was not only accurate, but somewhat prophetic. The land known as the "Amendment Beach Shares" and the "Bowling Saloon" is now the property of the Nantucket Yacht Club, and had the lady or her heirs been able to perfect her title, she would today own some of the most valuable land on Nantucket.

Many of the legal disputes on the Island stem from the peculiar state of titles on Nantucket arising from the common ownership scheme of the Proprietorship. The situation requires a knowledge of history as well as law to resolve. Many other disputes arise from the vague descriptions and plans recorded in the

Registry of Deeds, using homemade deeds, colloquial phrase-
ology, and mariners' bearings to describe vital points of refer-
ence. Entire sections of the Island were surveyed by retired mariners, using seamen's language and rusty compasses, taking their
bearings from "the big rock" or the "whale-bone marker," and
producing plans which would not "close up" geometrically and
can never be located on the ground. There are classics such as
the deed which ran from "the hole in the ice," and one with a line
from "a pile of stones near the beach to the place where my
sheep shed used to stand."

The Massachusetts Land Court was established in 1898, as a
specialized court to settle real estate questions, and since its in-
ception, the dusty confines of the Land Court have been the
scene of many monumental battles. As the value of land increased, the limited number of acres on the Island, the affinity of
the landowners for their heritage, and the confused state of Island land titles have made this court a familiar battleground for
Nantucket lawyers and litigants. The court was organized and
equipped with specialists prepared to decide any land disputes,
and over the years the Land Court judges have become the acknowledged experts on the land law in the state. They have
come to learn that Nantucket takes a lively interest in its lawsuits, and it is no wonder the learned judges often throw up their
hands in despair when they see "Nantucket, s.s." on the docket
and confront a courtroom full of determined islanders ready for a
fight to the finish.

For these Nantucketers there is no end to a lawsuit. It cannot be settled, for that would mean "giving in." They could not
face their family and neighbors with the report of any compro-
mise, and of course, no amount of money would ever be
sufficient for the claim they were relinquishing because somebody might make more money from it in the future. A trade of
land might occasionally settle the case, but each side would be
convinced he had been cheated in the bargain. There is a great
deal of personal pride involved, for each litigant is certain he
knows the location and extent of his land because his father or
grandfather showed him the boundaries, and the record title always leaves him plenty of room for argument. The Nantucketers
who have paid taxes for years on land bounded by "a dirt road, a

swamp, some pine lands, and other land of owners unknown," cannot be denied their claim of ownership to land which may exist anywhere on the Island, and it will take a long and weary trial to convince them their land has long since been conveyed, washed away, or unthinkable as it may be, gobbled up by some previous claimant. These plaintiffs always appear in court, clutching the yellowed parchment deed to their ancestors which they have preserved and treasured over the years for this great day when it would prove its value. Only after much coaxing and assurance of its return will they relinquish it to be examined by the judge, and they will never leave the courtroom without the original in hand.

The opponent of the man with the deed is the man who has farmed, fenced, or otherwise used the land for a minimum of twenty years, and has established his title by adverse possession. Rather than rely upon some vague and suspicious document, he produces witnesses to his labors. With the testimony of relatives, workmen, and neighbors, he begins to spell out his claim of dominion over the land, telling of years of plowing, berry picking, posting against trespassers, and paying nominal taxes on some land somewhere, identified as "outlands" by the Assessors.

The best proof of adverse possession has always been the fence. Many early cases upheld the rights of the man who could successfully maintain a fence against his neighbors for twenty years. Thus, one clever Nantucket litigant became the acknowledged expert on the "post and ribbon fence," a simple and economic construction consisting of scattered cedar posts loosely connected by a strand of ribbon wire. This veteran of the courts would invariably testify that he had built such a fence around the land twenty-five years ago, that most of the fence had rotted away, but he could still locate the posts, and, oh yes, he had a piece of the ribbon wire right here in his back pocket.

The Nantucketers who fought so hard to hang on to their land may have had their troubles with the law, but as long as they were steadfast in their purpose, they were usually successful. There were others, however, who made their own problems, which neither law nor lawyers could resolve. A man could use his wisdom and energy to make his fortune on the sea or upon the land, but very few could succeed in both elements. One man who tried was old Peleg Macy, who may have been an ancestor of William Hussey Macy. He is remembered today for being the owner and sole contractor of Peleg's Wharf, a small pier built into the harbor from Washington Street at the foot of Fayette Street, used mostly for landing coal and lumber. No trace of Peleg's Wharf remains today, for this hardy islander made the mistake of turning his attention from the glittering waterfront to the lonely landscape, with the following ironic result:

> In our juvenile hours,
> A good uncle of ours
> A high place 'mong our busy men filled;
> He had planned out a pier,
> And for more than a year
> Was collecting material to build.
>
> On his out-of-town tours,
> As he jogged o'er the moors,
> If a big stone appealed to his heart,
> He would stop his old nag,
> And though heavy to drag,
> Would lift the stone into his cart.
>
> By getting so many
> He saved a shrewd penny,
> Making even his leisure hours pay,
> And so went on collecting,
> Ne'er even suspecting
> That he himself might rue the day.
>
> 'Twas down south, near the Creeks,
> That he labored for weeks,
> Filling in there with stone, brick and wood,
> And hoped by his labors,
> With help from his neighbors,
> To build up his work firm and good.
>
> It served his turn well
> For a limited spell,
> But was rather a cobbled affair,
> And today, for his pains,

Scarce a vestige remains,
Of the wharf Uncle Peleg built there.

Later on, we are told,
When the good man grew old,
He bought commons in dividend lands,
And went out to explore
The divisions all o'er,
To learn what he'd got on his hands.

With his good friend Isaiah
He cruised here and there,
Riding over a good deal of ground,
But the shares were all mixed,
Corners couldn't be fixed,
For but few bound-stones were to be found.

Uncle Peleg, surprised,
Seemed in mind exercised;
Then after a while, lost in thought,
His eyes wandered round,
As though searching the ground,
But he still held his peace and said naught.

His friend Isaiah stormed,
As his vexation warmed,
"What thee's bought here I don't understand;
Bought a pig-in-a-poke?
But, indeed, 'tis no joke,
For thee never can locate thy land!"

Then with his wrath mixing hot,
"The man ought to be shot
Who has carried these bound-works all off;"
"I'll tell thee Isaiah;
It's my fault, I declare;
I've got 'em all down in my wharf!"

—WILLIAM H. MACY

On a small island, where every inch of sand has value and where land titles are jealously scrutinized, there remains an unusual and colorful area where history, tradition, and necessity combined to overcome the written law and "the intention of the settlor" as inscribed in the law books and land records. On the easternmost shore of Nantucket, there is a living memorial to the ability of the islanders to adapt the law to local needs, an entire village which grew outside the law and yet found ready acceptance among the Nantucketers, gaining increased vitality over the years. At the outset, the founding of Codfish Park was considered a nuisance and a disgrace, but tolerance and public opinion turned it into a haven of human rights and individual freedom.

The easterly end of Nantucket was early occupied by the fishing shacks and cottages of Siasconset, called "'Sconset" by the islanders. These buildings were all located on the bluff, high above the beach. In 1814 the 'Sconset Beach was so narrow that heavy gales washed over it, and one street on the edge of the bank disappeared. Thereafter, the shifting shoals and reefs offshore, so hazardous to mariners, barricaded the beach so the land below the bank continually increased through accretion. The Island, worn and eroded on the south and west, has actually grown on its eastern end.

From the earliest days, the fishermen of 'Sconset launched their boats into the surf and returned to the beach at the base of the bluff with their codfish. Their equipment was primitive: the traditional double-ended dory, the only boat capable of being launched and landed in the surf, the long hand-line codfish rig, jigged over the side and jerked into the boat with the flapping catch, and the long-shanked oars which required back-breaking labor to bring the boat home. Codfishing was done in all kinds of weather because it was the islanders' livelihood, and whenever the fish were biting, the men must put to sea.

James H. Wood, a lively and hardy veteran fisherman, once emerged from his dory in the midst of a winter snow storm to find a crowd of people awaiting him on the beach at Codfish Park, anxious to learn if he were still alive. Certainly, he stated, but it was getting so cold he had to dip his mittens in the salt water to keep them from freezing up. Why the excitement? He was informed that the temperature had dropped to five degrees below zero, and the harbor had frozen over.

When the dorymen of 'Sconset returned with their catch, the cod were fileted and stretched out to dry on the broad beaches below the bluff. The colorful and pungent sweep of beach below the bank in 'Sconset soon earned the name of Codfish Park. Along with the fish and the drying nets, the fishermen set up boathouses and shanties for their gear, usually casual, mobile constructions made from driftwood or leftover lumber.

Hand-lining for codfish is a chancy business, and, like the whaling business, it required a steady supply of willing men and a market for their product. Gradually both faded out, and the dorymen of 'Sconset disappeared from the beach. They were replaced by a group of people who found that Codfish Park provided the best low-cost housing on Nantucket; the buildings were available at a reasonable price and the land, believe it or not, was free.

When the Proprietors divided the land on the Island into shares and apportioned it among the early settlers, they excluded the beaches from their plans. In later years, large shareholders sought to acquire the beach lands, and in some cases actually traded in shares of the common lands for various areas of these "undivided lands." The great landowner and Island benefactor, Henry Coffin, obtained title to the beach at 'Sconset and, in a spirit of public philanthropy, decided to donate it for use as a public park. In 1886 he deeded the entire sweep of beach land to three trustees to hold the land in trust as a park for the benefit of the inhabitants of Nantucket. It was a noble idea, but it was an impractical one. The trust was unfunded, and the trustees were unpaid. Nantucket was in an economic decline, and the bother and expense of tending vast acres of dubious value did not appeal to the current sense of public priorities.

Within a few years, rustic shanties and humble homes began to encroach on the land below the bank. They were constructed from the old fishermen's shanties, from ruins of fallen structures and driftwood found on the beach. The houses were clustered around cart paths and alleys with no particular plan and the result was a rustic village of highly independent squatters. The ramshackle collection of shacks which developed into the village of Codfish Park was tolerated to grow and prosper. Despite occasional complaints about the crowded conditions below the bank, the Town never seriously considered any legal moves to recover its park land. The inhabitants of Codfish Park had no legal title to their land or houses, but their uninterrupted possession of the land for over twenty years soon ripened into title by adverse possession. Their holdings were always vaguely defined by existing fence lines or cultivated gardens, but since they had no deeds to the land, the Town Assessors usually exempted them from paying property taxes.

Of course, there were problems. If one wanted to sell his property, the buyer could receive only a bill of sale for the personal property, the house or garage on the lot, so the price paid was usually nominal. The banks would not grant mortgages upon such titles, so most conveyances went for small sums to friends and relatives. As time went on, the value of even the humblest shack in Codfish Park increased greatly. Furthermore, the beach at 'Sconset grew with accretion. Homes of more value were built, and modern economics demanded that the situation be placed on a sound legal basis. In 1938, inspired by the necessity of clarifying the owners' titles for tax purposes and of confirming the extent of the Town's remaining waterfront park, the Town finally made an attempt to straighten out Codfish Park. It was decided to prepare a large plan of the entire area and petition the Land Court to register the title to the Town of Nantucket, whereupon the Town would convey the house lots back to the recognized owners. It was a good idea, but, like Henry Coffin's, it did not work. The judge of the Land Court would not accept the proposal, and sent it back with orders that each individual owner must prove his own title, a lengthy and expensive proposition. Codfish Park had again defied the law and enjoyed another forty years as an independent duchy, without titles or taxes.

In the 1970s the situation was again re-examined, as more substantial homes and more affluent owners sought to secure their property in the Park. The only way to do it was by registration in the Land Court. Codfish Park soon swarmed with surveyors measuring their way around tiny shacks, picket fences, and rose bushes. The Land Court was bombarded with scores of plans and petitions, each one seeking to register lots thirty feet in width and containing buildings valued at $300. Each owner claimed title by adverse possession.

Original registration in the Land Court is an expensive and time-consuming process because the title to each lot must be examined in depth by a court-appointed title examiner. Since all the titles were the same in origin, could not one examiner do all the pending cases? the Court was asked. Again, the answer was no; each case must endure the same ordeal. All the Codfish Park cases dragged their weary way through the Land Court, the titles were examined and re-examined, the lawyers sent their bills, and the clients moaned and groaned at the expense and delay.

The law is a deliberate process and a Land Court decree of registration is a final judgment binding upon the whole world, so the Court does not render hasty decisions. On the other hand, judges like to clear their dockets and the Land Court judges are no exception. One of the modern Chief Judges of the Land Court recently set about to dismiss all the old cases which had been pending in his Court for many years. Scanning the list of ancient matters, he seized upon a pending case which was filed in 1923. "What!" he exclaimed. "This case was filed over fifty years ago!" The docket was lengthy, the original parties and lawyers dead and gone, but lawyer after lawyer had appeared to carry on the battle. Thinking he would get rid of this one in a hurry, he instructed his clerk to call the two remaining lawyers to tell them that the case should be settled or dismissed. Both lawyers responded with the traditional wail of the litigant, "Can you give us a little more time?"

Only time will cure the problems of the Park. The Land Court has imposed a heavy penalty on Codfish Park for its wayward ways, but Codfish Park has also taken its toll of the Land Court. It is not over yet, and we somehow believe that old Henry Coffin, who started it almost a century ago, is enjoying the spectacle.

II

Owners Unknown

"Do I hear two dollars for this fine parcel of land?" The auctioneer stood in front of the Town Treasurer's office beneath a drooping red flag, attempting to sell "tax title land" which the Town had taken for unpaid taxes, but he was having difficulty arousing any interest in the small group of listless bystanders who stood before him on this particularly hot July day of 1949. Nearby, some curious boys kept circling around on bicycles. Now and then they would dart off in search of more exciting pursuits, until the magnetic voice of the perspiring auctioneer brought them circling back again in fear that they might miss out on some momentous event.

Ordinarily these land auctions turned out to be non-events. They only took place when the Town fathers seized the land of delinquent taxpayers who repeatedly refused to pay their taxes. With all the necessary legal steps attended to, the land was advertised for public auction, the red flag was hung out, and the local auctioneer ascended the steps outside the Treasurer's office and banged his gavel. Common sense dictated that the auction should take place during the summer months when the prospects were strongest for securing some "off-island money," and the auction was always held in the middle of the day.

Most of the buyers were local speculators or Island lawyers, as the merchandise being sold was a suspicious commodity at best, and the prospect of purchasing a "tax title" did not excite many high bids. Most of the lots went quickly to a few bidders.

On this particular day, the weary auctioneer tried his best, but he rapidly reached the end of his list without making any remarkable sales, and the bored crowd started to drift away.

At this point some freshly arrived, off-island fun makers sauntered over from one of the many bars on Main Street. "What's going on?" demanded a voice from the newcomers.

"It's a land auction," came the answer.

"I'll buy it," bellowed the same voice. "I wanna stay on this island forever."

The small fry on the bicycles circled back again sensing a moment of high drama. The auctioneer, filled with renewed hopes, mopped his brow and took up his former position at his makeshift podium. With a flourish of showmanship, he waved his hand for attention and solemnly pronounced: "Gentlemen, we have one final piece of property for sale today, and believe me it is a corker! This beautiful estate is located on the South Shore and must contain a good ten or even twenty acres as far as I can see. It's the opportunity of a lifetime. What am I bid? What am I bid?"

"Ten dollars," rang out the same lively and unmistakable voice from the knot of newcomers.

"Better take it before he drinks it," seconded his chums.

"Do I hear more? Do I hear more?" queried the excited auctioneer.

"Better take his money, Henry," advised a retired salt who seldom left the Island. "Most of that land went overboard in the big storm last winter."

"Sold to the gentleman for ten dollars!" quickly shouted the auctioneer, bringing his gavel down with a resounding whack.

"Pay the Treasurer over there; cash if you please." A ten-dollar bill was handed over as the Treasurer signed a deed and delivered it to the proud owner.

"Now, if you'll just fill in your name and address on this sheet, here . . ." added the Treasurer amid the excitement.

At this fateful moment, however, the steamboat blew a piercing blast on the whistle announcing her immediate departure for the mainland and drowning out the Treasurer's words.

"For Christ's sake, you idiot, we're going to miss the boat," came a plaintive cry from one of the tourists as the Treasurer frantically waved the ten-dollar bill over the heads of the crowd, shouting: "Who bought this last one? Who bought this last one?"

Unfortunately, no one has ever been able to answer the Treasurer's question. Despite the large crowd which had been drawn in by the shouting, nobody could identify the purchaser and each of these eyewitnesses, or rather earwitnesses, had a different version of the transaction. Some said the purchaser's name was Smith, some said it was Small, and some said it was Sullivan. Everyone knew he was from the mainland, but no one knew whether he came from Springfield, Schenectady, or San Francisco. Some said that he was last seen weaving up the ferry's gangplank clutching a large Boston bag, but others said he had retreated back into a Main Street barroom and had refused to go home until the following day. Ever since, there has always been the chance that he would someday return to Nantucket and claim his land.

Legally speaking, the unidentified purchaser at the so-called steamboat auction became one of Nantucket's many owners unknown. Although his particular case was unusual, the reason why there are so many other owners unknown on the Island is easy to explain. When the sheep industry folded, Nantucket's outlying common lands became practically worthless, despite the ingenious attempts of Squire Coffin, and others like him, to put them to new uses. Because there was little or no market for the land, it was seldom sold, and few deeds were ever recorded in the Registry of Deeds identifying the successive owners. The land, originally held in common by many owners, was automatically and painlessly subdivided by inheritance into ever-smaller and more worthless shares until the heirs lost all track of their petty interests. In time they became owners unknown, even to themselves, and the real estate taxes on their land remained unpaid.

After World War II, the Town became exasperated at being unable to collect taxes on most of the Island's land because the owners could not be identified. To rectify this situation, the Assessors began to tax some of these parcels to John Doe, a fictitious person used when the names of the true owners remained unknown. After publishing a notice of foreclosure for nonpayment of taxes addressed to John Doe in the local newspaper, the Town would step in and take a tax title to the vacant land.

Following the foreclosure for nonpayment of taxes, the Town still did not obtain a good title to the land unless it went through a Land Court procedure which cut off the last rights of the true owners to redeem the land. This vital, final step in the Land Court was expensive, and the Selectmen refused to pay the Town Counsel to go to Boston and carry it out for fear of being criticized for paying to obtain worthless land. Instead, the Town would assign the tax titles, for a small sum, to anyone interested in buying them. The purchasers paid the back taxes, but all they had in return was a tax title. In order to perfect the title, so that a bank would give them a mortgage, they had to register the land in the Land Court at their own expense. By assigning the tax titles for a nominal sum, the Town accomplished several objectives: it collected some back taxes; it avoided the Land Court expense; it added another taxpayer to the tax rolls and more land to the assessed valuation of the Town.

In 1970 we embarked on a case which was destined to settle forever the centuries-old question of the Nantucket Sheep Commons. Our client, Frank Hardy, had purchased the tax titles to two parcels of land from the Town in 1967 for $34.36. After holding the land for three years, he petitioned the Land Court to have his land registered. The land was located in Share 3 of Nantucket's North Pasture, which was set off in 1821 to nineteen owners. These owners included seven Coffins, four Starbucks, two Folgers, a Macy, and the descendants of several other original Proprietors. Some of these nineteen owners had already disappeared by 1821 so the land was set off to their unspecified heirs.[1] In the Hardy case, the ghosts of the Nantucket Proprietors arose from their graves to do battle for the last time. The broad question at issue was whether or not the archaic, common ownership of the land, initiated by Tristram Coffin and his partners, could be legally terminated once and for all and the land transferred by the Town into individual ownership.

During the years between the original tax taking in 1966 and the filing of Hardy's Petition for Registration in 1970, many

[1] I.e., "heirs of William Starbuck," etc.

changes had taken place on Nantucket. An improved airport had made the Island more accessible to such places as New York City and Washington, D.C. Wealthy summer visitors appeared in increasing numbers seeking vacation homes. Inflation began to drive up land values, and the growing population found it more difficult to obtain land on which to live.

The road to financial success in Nantucket land speculation had proved a thorny one, as the sons of Zenas Coffin had discovered. Still it began to look as if Frank Hardy had come into a good thing, if the land could be registered in the Land Court. Those who had not been as farsighted or fortunate as Mr. Hardy in obtaining cheap tax titles questioned the whole procedure of taking these tax titles in the sheep commons and assigning them to specific individuals. They conveniently forgot to take into account the generations of bold Nantucketers who had died broke after investing in Nantucket land, and Hardy became the object of considerable jealousy.[2]

John Doe is no stranger to the law. He has been appearing regularly in court for centuries. The Massachusetts law recognized him and also recognized the practice of selling tax titles after John Doe assessments. The law did insist upon one very important requirement, however, before a John Doe assessment to common lands would be considered valid. If there was one common owner about who could be located by the Assessors, he was entitled to be assessed instead of John Doe, even if the other common owners could not be found. Thus, the narrow issue in the Hardy case was whether or not the Assessors had made reasonable efforts to discover at least one of the true owners before assessing the land to John Doe and selling it to Frank Hardy.

When Frank Hardy's case was tried in the Land Court in Boston, there were few persons present. At the last moment, however, a descendant of the original Proprietors appeared in opposition and produced a family tree in an effort to prove that she was

[2] Frank Hardy did not receive his land through a public auction like the steamboat auction. Land that was auctioned off was usually taken from known owners who simply didn't pay their taxes when billed. Land taken from unknown owners was considered too valueless to even go through the expense of an auction, so the Town Treasurer merely assigned these tax titles for a pittance on a first-come-first-served basis. When land values spiraled upwards, this procedure was questioned as serving "insiders." Later a state statute was passed requiring that all land taken for the nonpayment of taxes must be sold at public auction.

one of the true owners entitled to redeem the land upon payment of the back taxes.

"Your Honor, this goes back to 1659," declared her counsel popping up from his seat, and indeed he was correct. His client not only had a family tree to prove her point, copied from another, unidentified family tree which had fallen apart from age, she had a forest of family trees.

The Witness: This is my grandmother's family tree based upon one she had.

The Court: Based on your grandmother's records?

The Witness: I have pages from books I copied which show how I go back.

The Court: Was it a family Bible?

The Witness: No, there were books written about the people.

And so, back through the pages of Nantucket history we went until we reached Zenas Coffin, the witness's great-great-grandfather. It appeared that she was descended from Coffins, Starbucks, and perhaps from all the other original Proprietors, but she had no idea how much of Share 3 she owned or how she came by it. Soon after the hearing, she withdrew her opposition; her interest was obviously too infinitesimal to be worth the legal expense of establishing it.

Thus, the path to registration appeared clear for Mr. Hardy, but the judge in her opinion, after acknowledging the difficulties faced by the Assessors, said: "In a community as small, tightly knit and self-contained as Nantucket (at least during ten months of the year), the Court refuses to believe that with the exercise of reasonable diligence the Assessors would have been unable to find one actual owner."

So Hardy had lost. His tax titles could not be registered and he was stuck with the costs. Armed with the old saw that one page of history is worth a volume of logic and with a tattered group picture of the 500 Coffins at their 1881 reunion, we filed an appeal. Perhaps the picture would prove worth a thousand words. The Justices might come to realize that finding an actual owner was not simply a matter of looking up the name "Coffin" in the Nantucket telephone book. Our study of Nantucket had convinced us that the Assessors would never be able to ascertain the actual ownership of Share 3 without hiring a team of professional genealogists.

The case was reached in the Supreme Judicial Court shortly before Christmas 1975. We were reached for argument just before lunch. As the morning wore on, the Justices appeared to become grumpier and grumpier, dismissing appeals before the lawyers scarcely opened their mouths. Now it was our turn and we worried about the Justices' hunger pangs. As we started off, the High Court was deathly still, but soon broad smiles appeared on their faces and some of them broke into laughter as we held up the reunion picture. There was no need to go further. They had gotten the picture, and the picture was those rows upon rows of smiling Coffins at the 1881 reunion and the thousands upon thousands of owners unknown whom they represented.

The Court took a year to write its opinion, but we knew at the time of the argument that we had won. The Court held that, under the circumstances, the Assessors could not be reasonably expected to search beyond the Nantucket Court records for the actual owners of the sheep commons before assessing the land to John Doe.[3] The case was of considerable importance because, in the Land Court, an army of John Does from Nantucket was marching up to the counter for registration.

[3] *Hardy* v. *Jaekle,* 358 N.E. 2d 769 (1976).

12

Off-Islanders

The story of the law in Nantucket includes the tales of many notable men who found the Island a welcome haven during and after distinguished careers at the Bar. For reasons partly historical and partly geographical, the Island has always held a peculiar charm as a summer refuge for the legal profession. Perhaps this is due to the contrast between the peaceful Island and the conflicts and controversies which often filled their professional lives. In return for the seasons spent on their favorite Island, these men contributed generously to the lore of the law in Nantucket.

In the latter half of the nineteenth century, following the disaster of the Civil War and the disappearance of the whaling industry, Nantucket was at its lowest ebb, in both economy and spirit. Various business schemes were launched in an attempt to revive the Island, but all were short-lived and soon forgotten. Unlike the towns of the West, where a promising future was promoted by local entrepreneurs offering rewards for those alert enough to seize the opportunity, the Town of Nantucket seemed to drift backward into the past, with only its memories of the great days behind it and neither talent nor promise to brighten the future. The only hope for the Island, some suggested, was to establish itself as a summer resort.

In 1880 the noted New York attorney, Charles O'Conor, came to Nantucket, stayed at the Ocean House, and announced his intention to retire to "the finest and most healthful spot on the Atlantic Coast." O'Conor's opinions were respected; he was universally acclaimed "the profoundest lawyer to appear at the New York Bar." Born in New York City in 1804 of immigrant parents, he remained proud of his Irish ancestry and insisted upon spelling his name in the ancient form with one "n" instead of the more common form of "O'Connor." He casually explained the spelling: "Did you ever know an Irishman who could make both n's meet?"

As an attorney and public servant, Charles O'Conor gained fame for his defense of Jefferson Davis against charges of treason, for his lengthy and brilliant conduct of the Edwin Forrest divorce case, and for his part in the dissolution of the Tweed Ring in New York. When the citizens of New York protested the actions of William M. Tweed and his powerful political gang, Charles O'Conor was enlisted to lend both his legal talent and the prestige of his impeccable Irish background to the reform movement, which finally resulted in the destruction of the Tweed Ring, one of the great landmarks in American political history. Amid these accomplishments, O'Conor gained his own footnote in history, becoming in 1872 the first Roman Catholic to run for the Presidency. He was nominated by the American Party, or "Straight-Out Democrats," to oppose Horace Greeley and U. S. Grant.

The Island was visibly awed by the presence of the great O'Conor, and the newspaper reported in detail on the construction of his new mansion on the Cliff at Sherburne Heights overlooking Nantucket Sound. The lumber arrived by schooner, and the marble fireplaces were imported from Italy. O'Conor also erected a separate brick building to house his 18,000-volume library, reported to contain the finest private law collection in the country. The Island readers were informed that Mr. O'Conor had chartered the schooner *Onward* to carry his library from New York, and the complete job would require two or three trips. The completed mansion became one of the most familiar landmarks on the north shore of the Island.

Charles O'Conor's retirement years on Nantucket were brief, but memorable. He became a familiar figure in his long walks about town, with his tall, spare figure and finely chiseled Irish face, square chin, and white beard. Although the Nantucket Bar was anxious to add him to their ranks, he soon made it plain that he had come to Nantucket to escape clients. He did draft his own will and codicil, which survive in the records of the Nantucket Probate Court. (When he died, the great law library was returned to New York, along with his personal records of major cases.) Shortly before his death in 1884, Mr. O'Conor made a final gift to his adopted home town when he donated the sum of $7,000 to the Town of Nantucket, a gift intended to pay off the entire public debt of the Town, a fabulous sum in those days. Always the wise counsellor, he accompanied the check with a stern warning that the Town should never again fall into debt. Upon his death, the Island mourned him as a respected and beloved citizen, and the New York Bar Association memorialized him as ". . . the embodiment of the qualities, mental and moral, which should enter into and constitute the character of a great jurist and advocate."

Nantucket seemed to admire its visiting lawyers more than the local variety. As a community which had existed for years without lawyers, the Island did not take kindly to its early practitioners. The first commentator on the Nantucket Bar left little doubt on this subject.

The first notable author to visit Nantucket was a peripatetic Frenchman, J. Hector St. John de Crevecoeur who arrived in 1777, and made observations which gave most Europeans their first view of the new nation. In his *Letters From an American Farmer* (1792) he painted a glowing picture of the early islanders, living in a state of natural law which afforded them the personal freedom and economic opportunity denied their European contemporaries. Then he came upon the Island's lone lawyer:

> One single lawyer has of late years found means to live here, but his best fortune proceeds from having married one of the wealthiest heiresses of the Island than from the emoluments of his practice. . . . Lawyers are so numerous in all populous towns that I am surprised they never thought before of establishing themselves here. . . . What a pity that our forefathers, who

happily extinguished so many errors and abuses, both religious and civil, did not also prevent the introduction of a set of men so dangerous!

There is no bill of particulars attached to de Crevecoeur's polemic, and whatever this poor barrister had done to become the serpent in Nantucket's Garden of Eden will never be known. It is doubtful the local one-man Bar Association ever made a formal complaint. Court records indicate the subject of this attack was a lawyer with the Dickensian name of Phineas Fanning, the son-in-law of Keziah Coffin. Since Keziah's aggressive business practices had aroused the enmity of the Island, the lawyer who was assigned to foreclose her mortgages would never have won any popularity contest.

Colonial Nantucketers saw little need for the legal profession, but with the establishment of a settled government and the rising tide of the economy, the value of trained lawyers became apparent, even in Nantucket. When the cause warranted it, the islanders sought the best legal talent available, and in 1828 that meant the great Daniel Webster.

Aaron Mitchell, the leading Quaker merchant, had a case coming up before the Nantucket court and wanted to ensure his success; so he went to Boston and saw Webster in his Court Street office. "What will thee come to Nantucket for?" he asked the great lawyer.

"Fifteen hundred dollars," said Webster.

"That is an awful price," Mitchell protested.

"Well, it will take the whole week, and if I do, I would just as soon try every case on the docket," Webster replied.

"All right," said Mitchell, "I will engage thee."

Friend Mitchell then returned to the Island and asked each man who had a case what he would give to have the great Daniel Webster try it for him, then made a bargain at a fixed price for all those litigants who would pay the most. When Webster arrived he was met on the wharf by Mitchell and informed he was to try every case on the docket.

During the trial of one case, Webster asked a witness what he was doing during the time in question.

"I was putting a snoodle-dog in the deck."

"A snoodle-dog?" asked Webster. "And what may that be?"

"What!" exclaimed the sailor, "You, the Great Webster, maker of Webster's Dictionary, and you don't know what a snoodle-dog is?"[1] (A snoodle-dog is a wedge or a patch put into the deck or other surface to fill in a crack, a hole, or a worn place.)

As Webster was boarding the packet to return to the mainland, he asked Mitchell how he had come out on the deal. "Well, Friend Daniel, I will tell thee," was the reply. "I got my own case tried for nothing, and I cleared sixteen hundred dollars." Webster had argued and won every case on the Nantucket docket.

Nantucket attorney and historian Henry Barnard Worth was a man of great legal talent who contributed much to the Island's legal history. His practice in Nantucket led him into the study of the ancient land law, and he became the acknowledged expert on early Indian titles, sheep commons, and the proprietory system of land holdings. Because of his ability and scholarship, he was frequently called upon to render opinions to the Town which were so important that they were often reprinted in full in the *Inquirer and Mirror*.

Worth also had a lively interest in the Nantucket system of justice, and, following the celebrated Hilliard Case of 1919, wrote the following comments on the "Psychology of Nantucket Justice."

> You can't go to Nantucket with a brass band to arrest a criminal—and if you arrive with a corps of detectives and lawyers and stenographers, you can expect to be greeted with a united front of ignorance of any black deeds that have transpired on the Island . . . but that does not mean Nantucket justice is found wanting, nor that you can't convict a man of a crime in its courthouse or that honest men have ceased to exist on the Island . . . it simply means that practice on Nantucket is pursued in its individual way, which has seen it satisfactorily through two centuries, with a brand of public

[1] At this time Noah Webster, the originator of Webster's Dictionary, who lived for a while in Massachusetts and also served in the Massachusetts Legislature, was more widely known than the famous lawyer-statesman Daniel Webster.

ethics and morals as high in Nantucket as anywhere
else.

We are willing to match the Nantucket code of
morals, ethics and justice against the rest of the world
. . . all such criticism of the system has come from off-
Islanders who don't know the people they are criticizing
and would not understand them if they lived among
them for years.

The wisdom and insight of Henry B. Worth bears remembering
as good advice to both lawyers and laymen.

In 1924, the noted humorist, Irvin S. Cobb, visited the Island
where he loved to strut around in his colorful cap and knickers,
billing himself as "the worst golfer in America." He had a great
fondness for court houses and a fund of court-house tales
from his native Kentucky upon which he based his numerous
Judge Priest stories of country justice. He found a natural com-
panion in Judge FitzRandolph of the Nantucket District Court,
who would not hesitate to adjourn court for an hour or so while
they swapped stories. On one occasion, he regaled the court-
house crowd with his story about the young Kentucky law clerk
who presented himself before the local Bar Examiners for his oral
examination: he cautiously admitted he knew nothing about
Blackstone and had never read the Constitution, but, he insisted,
he was very familiar with the statutes of Kentucky. "Then you're
a fool!" shouted the examining judge. "The legislature is likely to
meet and repeal everything you know!"

As Nantucket gained fame as a vacation spot, it became
more popular with the noted attorneys of the land, many of
whom became permanent fixtures of the summer colony, especially in the village of 'Sconset. Among those of recent memory
were Emory P. Buckner, U. S. Attorney for New York during the
Prohibition Era, Lee Parsons Davis, great trial lawyer and former
District Attorney for Westchester County, New York (who was
not above trying an occasional case in the Nantucket District
Court), and John Lord O'Brien, senior partner of Covington &
Burling and one of the great constitutional lawyers of his day.
The Island has been the home of Judge Whitman Knapp, who
headed the Knapp Commission investigation of the New York

Police Department before his appointment to the Federal Court; Clark Clifford, Washington attorney and Presidential advisor; and Arthur H. Dean, senior partner of Sullivan & Cromwell, who served many Presidents as special ambassador and negotiator in foreign relations. Mr. Dean's dedication to Nantucket resulted in his donation of hundreds of acres of land on the eastern end of the Island to conservation purposes.

One of the most popular visitors to the Island was Judge Eugene Hudson of the Massachusetts Superior Court, who first came to Nantucket in 1947 and returned many times both as a visitor and as the presiding justice at the semiannual Superior Court sessions. His favorite tale, often repeated, concerned his first visit; he was having his shoes shined on Main Street by a local lad who admitted he had never been off the Island. The judge, who had many social and political contacts in Boston thought it would be a great idea to bring to Boston all the local Nantucket boys who had never seen the mainland. He immediately sent the boy scurrying to round up all the others who had never been off-island, and, in due time, the trip was arranged. Twenty Nantucket lads took the steamboat and the train to South Station. They were lodged at the Parker House in Boston as the guests of the Ancient and Honorable Artillery Company. The boys had a great week in the city, visiting the State House, meeting the Governor, and taking in a Red Sox game at Fenway Park. After several happy days on the town, the boys left for home, with profuse thanks to the judge and the Ancients. Only then did the hosts find they had made one mistake with their Island guests: the homesick boys had run up several hundred dollars in long-distance calls to Nantucket.

The United States Supreme Court has been well represented on Nantucket in recent years in the presence of Justice William J. Brennan, Jr., who has regularly summered in a cottage on Old North Wharf. The personable judge became a welcome member of the Wharf Rats Club, where he was always willing to add his wit and wisdom to the conversation, while remaining within the limits of judicial discretion. On one occasion, as a young lawyer cornered him for a curbstone opinion on a doubtful point of law, the Justice admitted he did not know the answer. "Nevertheless," pressed the lawyer, "whatever you say, Judge, that is the law."

"Oh, no, it is not," said the Justice, shaking his head, "It takes five of us."

As Justice Brennan was leaving the Nantucket Atheneum library one afternoon, he was met on the sidewalk by a lawyer from the city, accompanied by his young son. The lawyer stared in amazement and said, "Your Honor, I am so suprised to meet you here in Nantucket . . . may I have the privilege of introducing my son to you. . . . Son, I would like you to meet one of the Justices of the United States Supreme Court, the highest court in the land. . . . Son, I would like you to shake hands with . . . Mr. Justice Stewart."

The acknowledged dean of the off-island lawyers was the noted New York attorney, Morris L. Ernst, who summered on Nantucket from 1927 to his death in 1974. For him, Nantucket was more than a summer resort, it was a way of life. He boasted about his two favorite islands, Manhattan and Nantucket, and seemed to thrive in both climates—although he often claimed it was the summer on Nantucket which enabled him to survive another winter in Manhattan.

Ernst's life in Nantucket was busy and fulfilling. In the early years, he spent time sailing and working with his hands, taking as much pride in a finished playhouse for his grandchildren as in a polished brief for the Supreme Court. He loved to mingle both the great and the humble, introducing Edward R. Murrow to the young editor of the *Inquirer and Mirror* and inviting the youngest lawyer in Nantucket to meet Edward Bennett Williams. His home became a haven for many noted guests, but was equally open to young students, writers, and lawyers with whom he shared his wisdom and hospitality.

Morris Ernst saw in Nantucket the values of the small-town life. As a student of Justice Brandeis, who constantly decried "The Curse of Bigness," Ernst treasured the ideal of the small community where the individual could make his voice heard. Years ago, he claimed that New York City was just too big to be governed because nobody cared what happened outside his own neighborhood. To him, the small-town life was the good life, and Nantucket was the ideal. He loved the informality and independence of the small-town law practice, and his standard advice to young lawyers was always, "Get out of the big cities; move to a small town near the mountains or the shore; you won't make much money, but your wife can always teach school, and you can go sailing or skiing and live longer."

While one of the authors was in the State Legislature, Ernst suggested that Nantucket, which seldom needed any large state construction projects, should use its state highway money for the construction of bicycle paths. In due time, the state's first bicycle path was built from Nantucket to 'Sconset. To inaugurate the project, we invited the eminent Boston heart specialist, Dr. Paul Dudley White. He came to Nantucket, cut the ribbon, and took the first bicycle ride on the path. Dr. White, who had gained national fame when he cared for President Eisenhower after his heart attack, was then the most famous doctor in the country and had long advocated bicycling as the most effective form of exercise for people of all ages. It was only appropriate that the great doctor and the great lawyer should meet each other. They had a wonderful time; the trim Yankee doctor in his three-piece suit, and the New York lawyer in his Bermuda shorts. "What did you talk about?" we asked later.

"Mostly bicycles," came the reply from Morris Ernst. "And I thanked him for keeping Eisenhower alive so that fellow Nixon would not become President."

It could only have happened on Nantucket.

13

Freehold in the Sea

Nantucket can take pride in the fact that this isolated, independent, and self-governing Island was a pioneer in recognizing the civil rights of its citizens, a tradition which has been well maintained to the present day. Although members of the Society of Friends applied strict rules within their own community, they demonstrated tolerance toward others and proved by example their belief in basic human rights.

The first settlers of Nantucket were a largely homogeneous aggregation of white men and women, many of them closely related by family and business connections. Although they were fiercely proud and protective of their Island home, they early displayed a sense of solicitude and compassion, which was unusual for that time, and in many ways proved themselves far advanced in the treatment of their fellow men.

From the earliest days, Nantucket was destined to become a leader in the field of women's rights, and the history of the Island abounds in examples of equality between the sexes. Indeed, it may be argued that in Nantucket the women were more than equal. This was again a result of the Quaker tradition; for, although the Quaker Meetings traditionally segregated men and women on opposite sides of the room, the women maintained their equality and importance before the Lord. During the whaling days, when men went away to sea as young teen-agers and were often away from home for three- or four-year voyages, women developed the independence and ability needed to manage the homes, farms, and businesses during their absence. Whaling was very much a family and community industry in Nantucket. The close family ties and dependence upon the success of the whaling voyages made it inevitable. Entire ships were often manned by sons, nephews, and cousins of one family. As it was the Nantucket boy's destiny to make his future on the sea, it was the Nantucket girl's responsibility to assist and encourage this enterprise. It was this successful combination of the determined Quaker whalers and dedicated women which produced the golden age of Nantucket prosperity.

There are many old tales about the independence of the Nantucket women. Traditionally, a Nantucket girl would not agree to marry her young suitor until he had taken his first whale; the poor landlubber who preferred the farm to the sea was often destined for a lonely life with the livestock. When the men went to sea, the women went to work in the shops and stores to sustain the families; for the whalers had no guaranteed wages, but received only a share or "lay" from the profits of the voyage. There were occasions when a husband returned to report, "We didn't catch a single whale, but we had a damn fine sail." At one time, most of the shops on Center Street were operated by women, resulting in the street's quaint name of "Petticoat Row." These women were very sharp and successful traders.

The first noted Nantucket businesswoman was Keziah Coffin, who began by selling pins and needles and running a "cent school" (one cent per child per day) while her husband was at sea, starting a business enterprise which grew and prospered. At the start of the Revolutionary War, she made no secret of her Loyalist sympathies. Her strong ties with the British enabled her to do a brisk business despite the blockade of the Island. In return for shipments from the mainland, which amounted to a virtual monopoly, Keziah granted loans and credits for which she took notes and mortgages on many Nantucket homes and vessels. She acquired a country home in Quaise and a town house on Center Street. Her aggressive acquisitions and financial success earned her many enemies on the Island, and when the Revolutionary War ended, the Nantucketers united to do her in.

Keziah Coffin had a daughter who married the only lawyer on the Island, a barrister named Phineas Fanning. He was probably the object of the diatribe written by de Crevecoeur after his visit in 1777. Keziah turned her legal business over to her son-in-law with orders to foreclose every mortgage on the Island. The Nantucketers promptly contested every case. When the properties went to foreclosure sales, it was arranged that only one buyer would appear to bid them in far below value. Although she was never a popular figure, many thought her to be victimized by the local courts. True to her business principles and battling to the end, Keziah Coffin spent the last day of her life testifying in court in 1798, then dragged herself home, fell backward down the steps, and died of a broken neck.

Two other early examples of more noble character made themselves famous, one as an advocate of women's rights, and one for her scientific achievement. Lucretia Coffin Mott (1793–1880) was born on Fair Street in Nantucket, moved to Philadelphia and married James Mott, by whom she bore six children. She became a minister of the Society of Friends and one of the earliest and most important pioneers of women's suffrage. Maria Mitchell (1818–1889) was the daughter of the cashier of the Pacific National Bank and developed an early interest in mathematics and astronomy. From a homemade observatory on the roof of the bank, she discovered a new comet in 1847, which now bears her name.

In later years, the women of Nantucket preserved Island tradition, most often in the role of teachers in the public schools. The industry and ability of the Nantucket women frequently led them to seek higher education in the state teachers' colleges during an era when very few women obtained college degrees. Several Nantucket teachers returned to the Island, where they contributed to the education of many generations of local children. Many others went on to become able and respected teachers in schools on the mainland, giving rise to the expression "The Island of Nantucket produces nothing except cranberries and school-teachers!"

In the twentieth century, the role of women in public life on Nantucket continued and expanded. This is especially true in the field of the law, for although the female lawyer is still a rare sight in many communities, Nantucket became a haven for several notable legal talents. In 1934 Ethel Mackiernan was appointed to the Nantucket District Court, the first female presiding justice in the State. Her successor, Caroline Leveen, presided over the Nantucket District Court for thirty-three years. The tradition was continued in 1975, when Governor Michael Dukakis appointed Elizabeth Dolan as Judge of Probate for Nantucket County.

Mention of memorable Nantucket women must include Grace M. Henry, who came to Nantucket as a young lawyer to work in the office of Judge Reginald T. FitzRandolph. She later became Clerk of the District Court and director of the Pacific National Bank. She was a member of the Massachusetts Bar for fifty years, greatly honored and respected by the people of Nantucket.

Much of the Island's tolerance stemmed from its maritime traditions, for the value of a man at sea did not depend upon his origin or color. Many of the Nantucket whalers called at the West Indies, the Azores, and the islands off the coast of Africa, where they often recruited crewmen and deckhands for their voyages. Upon returning to Nantucket, some of these men settled in the Town, in such numbers that the south part of Nantucket Town acquired the name of Guinea. The little street now called Angora was formerly Angola, and on the corner of York and Pleasant Streets there was erected in 1831 the York Street Colored Baptist Church. It was later used as a school for minority children.

Quakers were naturally repelled by the concept of slavery and the citizens and merchants of Nantucket demonstrated their sentiments early.

In the Elihu Coleman house on Hawthorne Lane, in 1730 the Quaker author Elihu Coleman wrote a famous tract "against the despicable practice of making slaves of men." This was the first Quaker anti-slavery commentary and served as a direct forerunner of the Abolitionist movement which flourished in New England.

On one memorable occasion in 1770, the great whaling merchant and leading Quaker, William Rotch, declared the freedom of Absalom Boston, a black mariner who had served on Rotch ships and demonstrated unusual nautical ability. Boston's former master came to Nantucket and attempted to regain possession of Boston as his personal property, but a Nantucket judge and jury declared him a free man. The owner, disgusted with Island justice, threatened to carry his case to an appeals court in Boston, but William Rotch retained the counsel of John Adams to handle the defense, and the matter went no further. Traditionally, Nantucket followed the example of William Rotch, and thereafter its Quakers never again kept slaves.

The grateful Absalom Boston became America's first black whaling captain, recruited an all-black crew, and sailed away into the Pacific as master of his own ship. Captain Boston's portrait now hangs in the Peter Folger Museum, a source of great interest to visitors and a lasting memorial to the humanity and justice of early Nantucket.

In 1822 a fugitive slave named Arthur Cooper who had settled on Nantucket was confronted by his owner on his very doorstep, but was rescued by an aroused mob and sheltered by the Quakers until his pursuers fled the Island.

William Lloyd Garrison, the fiery orator and editor of the *Liberator,* was the most prominent Abolitionist of them all, and no stranger to Nantucket. He frequently visited the Island on his lecture tours and fund-raising drives, for Nantucket was then at its peak as a whaling capital and ranked third behind Boston and Salem as a shipping port of New England. Garrison had many friends on the Island, not only among the Quakers, but also in the south end of Town known as Guinea, where an educated black man named Edward J. Pompey served as his Island agent for the *Liberator.*

In August of 1841, the Anti-Slavery Society advertised a series of meetings to be held in the Atheneum, the public library and lecture hall which served then, as now, as the seat of culture on the Island. The presence of Garrison and other noted Abolitionist speakers was widely advertised, and as the scheduled date grew nearer, rumblings of excitement and impending trouble swept the Town. Garrison's oratory had been the cause of violent reactions from both pro- and anti-slavery forces on the mainland, where many of his meetings had been disrupted by showers of fruit and stones, and the buildings themselves had been attacked and burned by angry mobs.

The proprietors of the Atheneum became anxious about the security of their beautiful building and the valuable collection of books and antiques entrusted to their care. They withdrew their offer of the building for the anti-slavery meeting, depriving the Atheneum of a glorious moment in the history of American civil liberties. Ironically, within five years, the Atheneum and its collection were burned to the ground in the Great Fire of 1846 which destroyed downtown Nantucket.

Undismayed, the Anti-Slavery Society looked about the Town for another hall, and after being turned down by other public meeting places, finally were offered the use of the "Big Shop" by the owners, George and Reuben Coffin.

The Big Shop stood on Saratoga Street, near Vestal Street, and was one of the most versatile and interesting buildings in Nantucket Town.[1] It was one of the largest buildings in town, and had been used as a wool market, fish market, and carpenter shop where boats, barrels, and whaling supplies for the Island's whaling fleet were produced. It became a popular gathering place for meetings of the most independent and open-minded citizens of the Island, gaining a reputation as a place where any person was free to stand up and speak his mind without fear or criticism.

On the night of Wednesday, August 16, 1841, the hall was filled to capacity. The vast majority of the audience consisted of Nantucket Quakers, soberly garbed in heavy gray and black, the men wearing broad-brimmed hats and the women in bonnets, although it was a warm and humid night. All sat quietly and attentively as the Nantucket Society elected its officers and the visiting Abolitionists were introduced: William Lloyd Garrison of Boston, Wendell Phillips, author and orator, Edmund Quincy of Boston, Parker Pillsbury, Nathaniel Whitney, and the Secretary of the Anti-Slavery Society, John A. Collins.

Seated quietly in the audience with a group of off-island visitors from New Bedford was a tall, powerfully built young black man named Frederick Douglass. Feeling conspicuous and uncomfortable in the predominantly white audience of strange and silent Nantucketers, he slouched in his seat and stared grimly ahead at the speakers on the platform. The son of a white father and slave mother, for twenty-one years he had been a slave on a southern plantation. Three years before, he had escaped his

---

[1] The original building still stands on the corner of Quaker Road and Milk Street, where it is the home of Attorney and Mrs. James K. Glidden.

master, made his way to the coast, and aided by friends, had shipped to New Bedford, where, as a fugitive, he had changed his name from Bailey to Douglass.

Douglass had impressed his benefactors in New Bedford, for he had obtained some education in his youth and proved to have a keen intellect and a natural eloquence, which showed itself in talks to other black men in New Bedford. Deeply dedicated to the Abolitionist movement, he was uncertain of his role in it. He heard about the meeting and decided to go to the Island to listen to the orators, especially Garrison, who had afforded him much inspiration in the *Liberator*.

On the packet sailing to Nantucket, one of the New Bedford men spotted Douglass and asked him to say a few words at the meeting that evening. Pleased and honored by the request, Douglass agreed. Now, as he sat among the crowd in the Big Shop, all confidence drained from him; distrusting his ability to speak in public, he prayed that his friend would excuse him from his promise.

Garrison arose and offered two resolutions. The first was readily accepted, but the second, calling upon the people of the North to take a public stand in opposition to slavery, provoked some debate. The resolution was advocated by William M. Chase of Providence, Charles B. Ray of New York, Edmund Quincy of Boston, and Paul C. Howard of New Bedford. Each of these men was a noted reformer and seasoned orator, delivering ringing speeches which had thrilled audiences across the land. Douglass and the off-island visitors heard only a polite murmur of applause as each man finished. They were witnessing the response of a Quaker Meeting, where the members traditionally sat in strained silence until one felt "the spirit move him" to speak. No reaction was expected, for the natural calm and dignity of the Society of Friends prevented them from any show of enthusiasm in public.

Douglass's friend from New Bedford reminded him of his promise to speak and, signaling to the chair, prodded him toward the platform. Had he not promised his friend, he would never have attempted it; but now he found himself, trembling and embarrassed, standing before the meeting.

As Frederick Douglass looked down from the platform at the staid and solemn faces of these Nantucketers, he wondered why these emotionless, disinterested people, located far away from slavery and the agony of his race, living alone on this Island in the sea, should be interested in the story of a fugitive slave.

His words were, at first, inarticulate, and his voice trembled and stammered. The audience stirred uncomfortably. His eyes tried to avoid the gaze of the quiet people who sat in row after row staring at him. His powerful shoulders drooped, and his chin slumped to his chest. Momentarily he showed his audience the role he most wished them to see, his appearance speaking louder than words of the subjugation of his people, the crest-fallen figure of the black man in America.

At the sight of this tall, powerful figure, so confused and humiliated, the sympathy of the fair-minded Nantucketers broke through the calm of the gathering, and a murmur of understanding rolled through the crowd to the ears of the embarrassed Douglass.

In an instant, he lost his confusion. His head lifted, his muscular figure became alert and commanding, and he began to speak, his words slow, deliberate, and pulsating with power. The tormented trickle of words was forgotten, and his speech became a swift stream of pictures and persuasion. He told them the story of his life as a fugitive slave. Before him, the audience stared in silence at the sight and sat in wonder at the sounds they heard, while behind him, the eyes of Garrison blazed with elation. Douglass spoke until the lateness of the hour forced him to close. His listeners responded, first with sympathy, then with amazement, then with excitement. When he finished and dropped his head in silence, the Nantucketers arose and gave him round after round of applause.

William Lloyd Garrison leaped forward on the platform and held up his hand for silence. He placed his hand on Douglass's shoulder and cried to the crowd, "Have we been listening to a piece of property—or a man?"

"A man!" the crowd shouted.

"And should such a man be held a slave in a republican and Christian land?"

"No! Never!" shouted the crowd.

"Shall such a man be sent back to slavery from the free soil of Massachusetts?" bellowed Garrison.

The Nantucketers were all on their feet, shouting and stamping wildly, "*No!* Never! No! No! No!"

Those quaint and quiet Quakers, those silent, staid, and unruffled Nantucketers, dressed in somber gray and black, who had sat calmly through an evening of oratory delivered by the most noted preachers and reformers of the day, stood in the Big Shop with flushed faces and waving arms, stamping and shouting their replies to the fiery questions, all because of the words of Frederick Douglass, who had delivered the first and greatest speech of his lifetime. Three years before, he had slipped into New Bedford as a fugitive slave, afraid to whisper his name. From this night on, his name would ring across the nation, for on this night, before an audience of quiet and cultured Nantucket citizens, he had delivered a speech so dramatic and powerful that his eloquence stirred the congregation to unbelievably wild enthusiasm.

When the meeting broke up, Frederick Douglass was immediately invited by John A. Collins to become a public speaker for the Anti-Slavery Society, and again declined from fear that his ability was inadequate to the task. But the powerful intercession of Garrison won him over, and again he agreed to give it a try. He became the most famous fugitive slave in America, an outstanding crusader for the Abolitionist movement, and a distinguished orator and author.

It was, indeed, a strange destiny which brought this fugitive slave to the Island of Nantucket, where the first principle of the anti-slavery movement had been advocated by a Nantucket Quaker. It was an even greater destiny which aroused this young black man, in the atmosphere of a Quaker Meeting, to feel "the spirit move him," to a speech which lifted him from obscurity to become a figure of towering dignity in his people's crusade for freedom.

14

High and Dry on
the Tight Little Island

The Noble Experiment of Prohibition arrived in Nantucket in 1919 and was received by the islanders with a combination of public support and private opposition which seriously strained the basically law-abiding attitudes of its people. At that time, the State of Massachusetts was one of the notoriously "wet" states of the Union, resolutely refusing to ratify the Nineteenth Amendment until almost every other state had fallen into line. This situation was usually attributed to the large urban, immigrant, and Catholic population of Massachusetts and its neighbor, Rhode Island. Nantucket, on the other hand, was mostly rural, native, and Protestant; yet the Nantucketers chose this period of national crusade and crisis to demonstrate their most arbitrary brand of Yankee independence, as if to tell the world that Nantucket would make its own laws, or at least choose them.

Toward the outside world, Nantucket had always beamed a calm and peaceable image: the Isle of Peace and Tranquillity, where the law was obeyed without question and the citizens would not have it otherwise. The Town had cheered enthusiastically for Prohibition, the churches rang with its praise, the voters clamored for Coolidge and Harding, and the staunch *Inquirer and Mirror,* which seldom editorialized, urged the voters to rally against the threat of beer for the working man:

The voters should vote NO on the referendum on the ballot next week . . . the voters should stand behind Governor Coolidge and show their disapproval of any legislation which tends to open the way to the saloon, even in a minor degree. . . .

The Prohibition Amendment would never have secured the ratification of 45 states unless it was desired by a large majority of the people . . . it has reduced drunkenness, has greatly cut down the jail population and is leading millions of men to spend their money on their families instead of for hot stuff to pour down their throats . . .

Regardless of the preachers and heedless of the editorials, the islanders treated the cause of Prohibition with the attitude of resignation and indifference usually afforded foreign wars and distant disasters. "Nantucket is a dry town and will continue to vote dry," quipped one local commentator, "just so long as the voters are sober enough to stagger to the polls."

Prohibition began in Massachusetts on July 1, 1919, but the citizen was free after that date to drink up whatever he had on hand before the deadline. In the spring of the year, it was noted the Island steamers were running unusually low in the water, and several passengers each day needed help in lugging their suitcases off the gangplanks. The *Inquirer and Mirror* noted: "From the appearance of the express packages brought to the Island each day, there will not be such a terrible drouth on Nantucket after all, even after July First."

Prohibition brought the Island face to face with its basic needs and desires, which often seemed very remote from those of the crusaders who had sold Prohibition to the nation. The year-round residents had the time and opportunity to indulge in any diversions they wished during the long winter months without adversely affecting their productivity or income. The summer population came to the Island from New York, Chicago, and Baltimore, intent on the pursuit of pleasure and seeking something to slake their thirst along the way. The decisive factor in the minds of everyone, they all agreed, was their location on an island of their own, far away from the source of this federal law and its powers of enforcement.

Without doubt, the summer of 1919 was fully as wet as any previous season on the Island. Many citizens thought Prohibition would not last long, and others had provided themselves so well they did not care whether it did or not. Thus was brought about one of Nantucket's most celebrated and controversial cases, the great 'Sconset Liquor Case.

'Sconset was the summer home of the noted actor and playwright, Robert Hilliard, a popular member of the summer actors' colony, who was famous as a matinee idol in the theater and as a fashionable figure among the village's summer folk, noted for his "flashy bathing suits, Panama hats, and huge button-hole bouquets." In the fall of 1919, Hilliard closed his summer home in 'Sconset and headed south to Baltimore for the winter. In doing so, he made a fateful decision to leave behind on the Island his choice pre-Prohibition cellar of scotch, Bourbon, and wine, valued at $3,400 in those gay tax-free days. The decision was a sensible one, prompted by a combination of habit, circumstance, and security; since he had always left his summer supply on the Island, he continued to do so; since the private transportation of liquor required government permits and red tape, he could not be bothered. (One must wonder what he had ready for the winter in Baltimore.) Most important of all, his stock was safe, for it was securely stored in the third compartment of his full brick cellar, behind four padlocked doors on grounds daily patrolled by his faithful Nantucket caretaker. Finally, of course, it was all on Nantucket, the quietest place on earth.

Before Hilliard reached Baltimore, his entire stock of liquor was gone. In those days, $3,400 worth of drink would fill several trucks, and 'Sconset was a quiet town with no traffic to speak of. But all had vanished without a trace or a sound. The stunned caretaker found nothing but broken locks, empty cases, and a few miserable bottles of second-rate goods remaining from the valuable cache. Summoning his courage, the poor caretaker rang up the operator and conveyed the tragic news to Baltimore. Robert Hilliard rose up in wrath, swore eternal vengeance upon the culprits, and promised to hire detectives to scour that Island and find his private stock. Not only were his goods valuable, but now they were irreplaceable. This had to be an inside job, he deduced. Hilliard returned to the Island to lead the search, but he was met with nothing but sympathy and suggestions, for, as one of the natives ruefully reminded him, "You can leave a thousand dollars in your house beside a bottle of whiskey, and on Nantucket a thief will take the bottle and leave the bills."

The Island buzzed with rumor for months. Everybody had a story and several accusations were made; it was said the police knew the culprit but would not act; it was even thought that certain figures around the court house knew the whole story but were keeping it quiet. A scandal was brewing while the bottles were emptying. Many of those empty bottles were turning up close to the grocery store of Larry Welch, who ran a small shop near the Town Pump in 'Sconset. The Chief of Police, Houghton Gibbs, had been suspicious of Welch for some time, especially since he came from Framingham and persistently remained in 'Sconset far beyond the usual grocery season. Finally marshaling his evidence, the chief polished up his badge and took a taxi ride out to 'Sconset, where he arrested Larry Welch on a charge of making illegal sales of liquor.

Now the Town warmed up for the great 'Sconset Liquor Case and the first big trial of Prohibition enforcement on Nantucket. Not since the days of the Great Bank Robbery had Nantucket looked forward to such a promising criminal trial, and everybody awaited the start of the action. Although the charge against Welch did not mention the Hilliard robbery, the whole Town knew it was Hilliard money behind the prosecution, especially when a lawyer arrived from New Bedford to prosecute the case "on behalf of the Chief of Police." Both the Presiding Justice and Special Justice of the Nantucket District Court disqualified themselves from hearing the landmark case, with no reasons given, and Judge Paul Swift from Barnstable gallantly sailed over to hold court on Nantucket. The Town grumbled, "We pay two judges and a clerk to hold Court all year, and the minute a big case comes up, they send for a feller from the mainland. Is that justice?"

The great trial began on a frigid day in December at 4:00 P.M., after the arrival of Judge Swift on the late boat. Reporters from New Bedford and Boston arrived with him, for the Hilliard name and Nantucket justice had given promise of a newsworthy trial. The small courtroom above the Pacific Club was so crowded with spectators that late arrivals could not enter and early arrivals could not leave. Striding dramatically through the crowd, Robert Hilliard made his most dramatic appearance, whirling off his Elizabethan cape and deploying his forces about the room with sweeping directions.

Hilliard sent his detectives to the stand and beamed triumphantly at their testimony, while Judge Swift peered suspiciously at the entire performance. Finally, the chief of police presented his star witness, Gus Pitman, a 'Sconset character who spent his summers picking up scraps of paper from the dusty lanes of the village, an occupation which left him tired and thirsty all winter. Yes, Gus admitted, he had bought a bottle of scotch from Larry Welch and paid him eight dollars for it—no bargain price in those days. Welch had produced the bottle from inside his barn and handed it to his parched customer. Gus was shown an empty bottle, which he quickly identified by the hayseed clinging to it.

Question: "When did that bottle become empty?"

Answer: "When I finished it."

Question: "When was that?"

Answer: "When I took the last drink."

Question: "Then what did you do with the bottle?"

Answer: "I carried it around and took occasional smells from it during the week."

The judge sat through the testimony without comment, but Robert Hilliard could not resist the opportunity to announce, at the end of the prosecution's witnesses, "There is your evidence!" as he whirled his cape and beamed at the Bench. Judge Swift was unimpressed as he announced, "I find the defendant Not Guilty for lack of corroborating evidence."

As the crowd rushed forward to congratulate Larry Welch and make their individual plans for celebrating this triumph of justice—a celebration undoubtedly supplied by the unhappy Hilliard—the great thespian sat fuming with rage. Hilliard announced publicly that he would never again return to this Island, but he soon overcame his disappointment, and when another summer rolled around, the familiar Panama hat and great boutonniere were again sighted arriving on Steamboat Wharf. So appreciative were the islanders of the quality of Hilliard's goods and the great times he had provided the Island that his return was marked with genuine enthusiasm, and Robert Hilliard found he now had more friends than ever before on Nantucket.

Nantucket's location made it a natural rendezvous for rumrunners from Canada, the Bahamas, and elsewhere. Rumrunners were small, fast vessels, many of them surplus ships from World War I which, stripped down for maximum speed and cargo capacity often outran the Coast Guard and other federal officials through the tricky channels and constant fogs around the Island. Once their cargo was brought ashore, there was no lack of able Nantucketers and thirsty consumers to facilitate its disposal. Many an isolated farmhouse or fishing shanty acquired a new popularity with the neighbors. One of the authors still lives in an old farmhouse strategically located across from the Creeks, which provided an excellent landing place on the edge of Town. This old farmhouse, with its surrounding barns, sheds, and willing farmers, became a treasure trove for the needy once the unscheduled goods arrived from the Creeks. During the 1920s, there was installed in the upstairs bedroom a complicated false fireplace which concealed a small room just the right size to hold hundreds of bottles of illicit beverages snug in their beds of burlap and straw. The fireplace itself was secured by electric locks which could be opened only by pressing a secret button located in a window frame and well concealed from view. The whole rig was installed by an electrician brought to the Island for that purpose and sent home on the next boat. Although the farmhouse had only naked light bulbs for illumination and a two-hole privy for plumbing, the electric fireplace was considered a good investment and served its purpose without detection until Repeal.

The mariners and fishermen of Nantucket had even more freedom of movement than their landlocked brothers, and when, in 1921, the greatest of the rumrunning schooners, the famous *Arethusa*, appeared off No Mans Land near Martha's Vineyard, many local lads sailed out to make her acquaintance. The *Arethusa* was a speedy yacht, purchased in Gloucester by the celebrated skipper, Bill McCoy, and fitted out with new engines and gear to carry thousands of cases of the very best imported goods from Nassau to the "Rum Row" of ships riding beyond the three-mile limit off the shores of New York and New Jersey. Bill McCoy's wares were reputed to be the best available; it was said that he always carried the "real McCoy goods," thus he earned a reputation for integrity in the trade and gained immortality in the language. On this occasion, his vessel landed thousands of cases of liquor on the Vineyard, but the authorities swarmed over the beaches and the desperate islanders were forced to hide the cases in a creek. By the time the authorities disappeared, the labels had washed off all the bottles, and customers were reluctant to pay top prices for the naked bottles. The problem was solved by Yankee ingenuity and modern merchandising when each customer was offered one free swig from the bottle to convince him he was, indeed, buying the real McCoy.

Geography placed Nantucket Island in the middle of the offshore rumrunning trade. Standing like a beacon in the midst of the heavy shipping lanes from Canada and Europe, the Island was practically surrounded by modern buccaneers from the Bahamas and the West Indies. By 1921 there were twenty-one rumrunners hove to off Block Island, ready to do business. Whiskey from Canada, scotch from Britain, and rum from the Indies washed ashore by the bottle, barrel, and case, threatening the tiny island with a tidal wave of illicit booze. The staunchly dry *Inquirer and Mirror* lamented:

> It may be a rather tender subject to touch upon, but nevertheless, we are going to pass the opinion that Prohibition as applied to Nantucket Island has been nothing but a farce. It is common knowledge that liquor has been obtainable here the past summer with little effort. . . . There is no one in authority to enforce the Federal laws.

Although the people of Nantucket continued to support the cause of Prohibition publicly, backing it in a 1924 referendum by the healthy margin of 394 to 191, they never felt themselves responsible for enforcement of the law. The whole matter was considered a federal problem, brought on by federal law and worthy of federal enforcement. Certainly, the Town police force of three men (one on days, two on nights) was not supposed to guard fifty miles of open beaches. Thus the Town cheered a new Coast Guard offensive against the liquor trade, using twenty World War I destroyers, 178 fast patrol boats, and 2,245 officers and men. The Coast Guard arrived in force on the Island, and one Nantucketer was convicted for selling a bottle of Green Stripe Scotch to a Coast Guard officer.

The life of the local police officer during the days of Prohibition was a busy one, with moments of high drama alternating with incidents of low comedy. Faced with the difficult task of enforcing an unpopular law under impossible conditions, they did their best.

The South Beach area, modern Washington Street, was then a nest of poor fishing shanties housing some of the Town's most troublesome characters. Acting on a tip, Officers Lawrence Mooney and Charles Chadwick raided a notorious shack which they described as a "nasty, dirty place, smelling of liquor," serving as weekend quarters for three men and "three young ladies from New Bedford." One of the owners of the shack, shocked at being singled out for attention, undertook to defend himself in District Court, and asked the officer why the police had raided his lodgings. "Well," Officer Mooney replied, "anytime the police get a call to look for a missing husband, that's the first place we look, and we always find them, either wholly or partly stewed." The owners got three months in jail, and the girls got one-way tickets back to New Bedford.

The Nantucket police brought their share of prisoners to court where Judge Reginald T. FitzRandolph presided and always sought to temper justice with both mercy and a touch of humor. Since these were the days of the great crusade, it was often standard practice to release a drunkard on his solemn vow to "take the pledge" and stop drinking. One local character, hauled in for his third offense, was being reprimanded by the judge for his failure to comply with his two previous promises to take the pledge. Fearful of being sentenced to the dusty confines of the Nantucket jail, the poor soul begged for one more chance, saying, "I'm willing to take the pledge, Judge, but my health will not allow me to refrain from liquor entirely."

The *Inquirer and Mirror* reported that State Police Officer Frates and Patrolman Lawrence Mooney brought Stanley Rowley into the court with a collection of items seized in a raid on Milk Street, consisting of two quarts of Old Tom gin, six quarts of Old Smuggler and two gallon wine jugs containing an unidentified homemade beverage. The trial was held on a hot day in July, and the issue turned on the potency of the contents of the jugs. While the defense attorney was arguing that the jugs contained a harmless brew with no kick to it, one of the jugs exploded and the entire contents hit the ceiling of the courtroom. This proved to be a colorful demonstration of the power of the local brew, and everyone in the courtroom (except the defendant) enjoyed a good laugh.

The ingenuity of the bootleggers was unlimited, and it took clever police work or luck to keep up with the enterprising importers. In 1926, illegal spirits arrived in hot-water bottles, which were quickly sniffed by Chief Houghton Gibbs and confiscated on Steamboat Wharf. In 1927, the police watched a new Hudson touring car struggle off the steamboat and head up Broad Street until its frame buckled under a load of twenty-three cases of whiskey.

If their methods were ingenious, their alibis were outrageous, and the Nantucket District Court heard them all with amused tolerance. When Officers Mooney, Charles Chadwick, and William Henderson raided the waterfront establishment of Willie Davis and seized 121 bottles of liquor, Mr. Davis stoutly denied that he was in the business of selling liquor, but was only keeping those bottles handy for his friends. Unfortunately, he could not remember any of their names. A few years later, the same Willie Davis was nabbed by the State Police lugging four gallons of moonshine liquor along Easy Street and was hauled before the court. Another terrible mistake, claimed Mr. Davis. The alcohol was not for drinking; he needed it for body rubs. Since the defendant was now over seventy years of age, the court told him to find another line of work and put him on probation. By 1932, the first illegal liquor arrived by plane, and the State Police seized ten cases of it on the primitive airstrip at Tom Nevers Head, while a number of thirsty citizens waited expectantly for their heaven-sent provisions.

The Prohibition years were not all fun and games on the Island; there was a good deal of money involved in the business and some of the players could get rough. In 1932 a particularly terrifying experience was visited upon Carl West, a popular black taxi driver who was known to everyone in Town and reputed to be an informer for the local police. One evening West was called to drive three men over the rutted roads near Gibbs Pond. Many miles from the nearest dwelling, he was slugged by one burly passenger, and beaten, bound, and gagged. His captors told him, "We were sent down here to get you; we are getting $500 for this job and we mean business. After we get through with you, we are going to get that bald-headed cop, Sergeant Mooney." West was then driven around the Island in the darkness, while his captors threatened to throw him into the surf, if they could find it. After many hours of terrifying captivity the assailants tired of the game and drove him into Prospect Hill Cemetery where they left him bound, gagged, and stripped to his shorts, propped against a gravestone. Somehow he managed to work himself free and raced to the police station, where Sergeant Mooney took care of him. Acting on his information, the local police quickly rounded up the three assailants. Two of them were locked up and eventually sent to State Prison, while the third, an illegal immigrant, was deported from the United States. Carl West and Sergeant Mooney remained the best of friends ever after.

In 1932 the local police raided the largest and most ingenious still ever discovered on Nantucket. Unfortunately, it was found in the pine lands off Polpis Road owned by Sergeant Lawrence F. Mooney. Any embarrassment felt by the officer was quickly forgotten in the popular admiration for the sheer magnitude of the enterprise, which became a local tourist attraction. Tracking a solitary figure along the Polpis Road in the early morning hours, the police noticed him turning into the pine woods near the duck pond south of the Mooney farm. Officers Mooney, Charles Chadwick, and Bill Henderson searched the woods until they discovered an open hatch in the pine floor of the forest which led to the bootlegger's bonanza. Beneath the ground was a fully equipped room, ten feet square and seven feet high, planked, floored and timbered, and covered over with a solid roof of thick pine thatch and newly planted pine trees. Inside the room they found a kerosene stove, copper boiler, three hogsheads full of steaming mash, and 100 gallons of prime moonshine ready

Peter Folger, justice of the peace, agent for Marine Underwriters. Portrait by Eastman Johnson, 1886. (*Nantucket Historical Association*)

Captain Charles Myrick, retired whaling captain. Portrait by Eastman Johnson, 1879. (*Nantucket Historical Association*)

Charles O'Conor, Esq., attorney and summer resident. Portrait by Mathew Brady. (*Nantucket Historical Association*)

Henry Barnard Worth, Esq., attorney, author, and historian. (*Nantucket Historical Association*)

Allen Coffin, Esq., Nantucket attorney. (*Nantucket Historical Association*)

William Hussey Macy, 1826–1891, Nantucket historian and author. (*Nantucket Historical Association*)

Nantucket Indian artifacts. (*Nantucket Historical Association*)

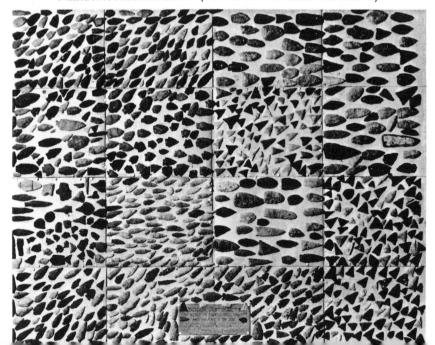

Nantucket Courthouse, 1965. (*Photo by W. Frederick Lucas*)

Chadwick's Folly

William Coffin, Nantucket banker, postmaster, and defendant. (*Courtesy of The Coffin School*)

MARY DYER

QUAKER

WITNESS FOR RELIGIOUS FREEDOM

HANGED ON BOSTON COMMON 1660

"MY LIFE NOT AVAILETH ME
IN COMPARISON TO THE
LIBERTY OF THE TRUTH"

Mary Dyer (*Photo by Richie Simpkins*)

General Hooker and his horse. (*Photo by Riche Simpkins*)

for delivery. Beneath the room was a thirty-foot well, reaching into the underground water needed for the process and fully lined with barrels for its entire depth. It was speculated that many men had a hand in the construction which involved removal and disposal of tons of earth without any visible trace. Bill Henderson later recalled this find as the largest bootlegging operation on the Island and claimed the operators made a lot of money from it before the bubble burst. The only man found at the scene was a Brava (Portuguese) who was quickly dispatched to the House of Correction, while the *Inquirer and Mirror* marveled that such an extensive operation could be constructed and operated by "an ignorant Brava." To Sergeant Mooney and the officers fell the sad task of filling the well and closing down the last still on Nantucket.

The repeal of Prohibition in 1933 ended Nantucket's most colorful illicit caper. As if suddenly eager to catch up with the rest of the country, the Town of Nantucket, which always "voted dry and drank wet," reversed its pattern on June 13 and voted in favor of local liquor licenses, 396 to 34. Undoubtedly, many of the voters had developed a taste for the forbidden fruit during the long dry spell. Prohibition as a crusade had proven to be an expensive failure for the nation, and, by making lawbreakers of a large segment of the population, had encouraged a disrespect for the law and its enforcement in every part of the society.

It must have been a great day when crowds hurrying down Steamboat Wharf heard the cry, "Here it comes, boys!" and a wagon rolled off the boat carrying Nantucket's first legal drink in many years: three cases of beer.

15
Justice and Justices

Judge Frank Smith had finished his instructions to the Nantucket jury and sent them out to consider their verdict in a civil case for money damages. The judge was a good-natured veteran of the Massachusetts Superior Court, but he had never before held court in these surroundings. As the Town and County of Nantucket had no real court house before 1965, the trial was being held in Bennett Hall next to the Congregational Church. The hall was used primarily for social events and athletic games, so the trial was held on the basketball court, the judge presided from the elevation of a five-foot stage, and the jury was locked up in a windowless shower room. When Judge Smith retired to his chambers in the church kitchen, he suddenly found he could hear every word of the jury's deliberations through the paper-thin walls.

The first voice heard was clearly that of the foreman, who asked, "Well, how much money are we going to give this guy?"

A juror replied, "Remember, the judge said we should consider all the evidence, weigh it carefully, and take our time to reach a just decision."

To this the foreman responded, "To hell with that old bastard! Thank God we don't have to listen to him anymore. And remember, he comes from the mainland!"

The judge took it all in good spirit and never forgot his lesson in the workings of the Nantucket jury system

Nantucketers have always shown an obvious distrust and

avoidance of the existing legal establishment. They have preferred to settle their own disputes, insofar as possible, by arbitration, custom, and agreement. This preference was historically attributed largely to the Quaker rule of the Island, which dictated that no Quaker could sue his brethren in court and which despised the paid advocate as much as the paid preacher. Thus, the islanders, from the foundation of the colony in 1659, managed most of their problems without trained lawyers until the famous trials arising from the Nantucket Bank Robbery in 1795. Off-island attorneys were summoned to resolve the bitterness because the pressures and emotions aroused by the robbery of the local bank threatened to divide the entire community. This independent tradition continued through the nineteenth-century sheep war and land controversies, which often reached a pitch of acrimony that left no islander neutral.

Indigenous justice was preferred and often required by the inhabitants of the Town. Brave and independent mariners, accustomed to obeying only their autocratic captains, were not about to take orders from any petty magistrate in their home town. Their women, entrusted with the responsibilities of home and business for extended periods while the men were at sea, did not need lawyers or judges to govern their daily pursuits. Thus, for many decades, the townspeople managed to live and prosper without resort to any formal legal establishment, and most of the old-timers thought it better that way.

Nantucket administered its own brand of justice before there were courts, and after the establishment of the courts, life continued much the same way. The force of public opinion was sufficient to keep the peace and see that justice was done. For session after session of the court, the judges could find no business to handle, the grand jury reported no indictments, and, after the judge congratulated the Island on its purity, everyone called it quits for another year. The Island had plenty of petty crime and drunkenness, but the offenders received such powerful signs of disapproval from their fellow townsmen that they seldom dared to take the chance of facing them in court. For more than two hundred years, Nantucket Island managed to operate a judicial system in which judges were usually men of great ability and wisdom, but completely untrained in the law. Walter Folger, a mathematical genius of exceptional versatility who had no formal legal education, presided over the Court of Common Pleas for six years, and never had one of his decisions appealed.

During the Island's first two centuries, the Nantucket Probate Court had only two judges who were members of the Bar. This position was considered a great honor and was often filled by a retired whaling captain. The most famous of these was Thaddeus C. DeFriez, who retired from thirty years at sea to give the court one of its most intelligent and successful administrators. His judicial decrees were fine examples of wisdom and clarity, perhaps due to many years' experience in writing his ships' logs.

Few officials were ever launched upon a judicial career more abruptly than George Cobb, who held the office of Clerk of Courts for thirty-seven years. Benjamin Gardner, who was Clerk of Courts for many years, was one day confronted by a reluctant witness who refused to take the oath before his testimony and asked to be allowed to affirm under the penalties of perjury as the Quakers were allowed to do. It was shown to the judge that this man had never before refused to take an oath, and in fact, "was frequently addicted to swearing when there was no occasion for it." The judge impatiently rapped his gavel and ordered the clerk to administer the usual oath. Clerk Gardner turned toward the bench and solemnly announced that he could not in good conscience compel a man to swear against his will, and that he would rather give up his job than do so. The judge removed the clerk from office, then turned to the sheriff and said, "Go get George Cobb."

Cobb was hard at work in a cooper's shop forging iron bands around whale-oil casks when the sheriff arrived, out of breath, to announce that Cobb was the new Clerk of the Court of Common Pleas. He finished his barrel, washed his hands, rolled down his shirtsleeves, put on his coat, and walked up to the court house, where he calmly administered the oath and began a long career. He managed the business of the court with dignity and efficiency and gained great respect and honor in the community.

The District Court of Nantucket, which hears all misdemeanors and minor civil cases, was first established in 1918 when the Governor appointed as its first presiding justice a popular attorney named Reginald Taliaferro FitzRandolph, a man who had become the youngest trial justice in the state upon his appointment to that position in 1910. Judge FitzRandolph was a hearty, convivial man who lived life to the fullest and dispensed justice without losing his sense of humor. He served as Moderator at the Town Meetings, and doubled as Santa Claus at Christmas. To this genial judge fell the burden of enforcing the Prohibition laws and he meted out justice with great devotion to the letter, if not the spirit, of the law. Many a night the Nantucket police encountered His Honor weaving across the cobblestones of Main Street and transported him safely back to his home in the early morning hours only to witness him ascend the bench at 9:00 A.M., bang his gavel, and solemnly announce, "This Court will not tolerate drunkenness in the streets of Nantucket!"

In those days, the local judge often had many functions. Judge FitzRandolph served as Town Counsel, Moderator, bank director, and delegate to the State Constitutional Convention. He also ran his private law practice from the dusty confines of the Pacific Club Building, but his busy schedule never interfered with his sense of humor, even when the joke was on him. One year a local lad of nineteen took a law school correspondence course, and the school wrote to Fitz to collect its bill for $66. When the judge told the boy he would have to pay it, the lad replied, "I read only a couple of chapters in those law books, but in one of them I found that a minor is not liable for his bills."

The Town mourned the untimely death of the judge in 1934.

He was followed by Miss Ethel Mackiernan of Boston, who was appointed by Governor Ely as the first female justice in the state. Her tenure lasted less than a year, for Nantucket was in the depths of the Depression and the natives proved very restless indeed. She was forced to listen to the lurid details of a series of sex crimes involving sodomy, bestiality, and incest. Shocked and dismayed, Judge Mackiernan resigned from the bench and returned to other aspects of the law, sadder but wiser in the ways of the world.

The modern judges have their own procedure for disposing of such crimes, which seem to be indigenous to isolated and rural communities. Superior Court Justice Francis W. Keating, faced with a farm lad charged with molesting a heifer, came up with the best solution for all concerned when he commented, "It is my practice to dismiss these charges, provided, of course, that the parties are willing to get married."

In 1934 Massachusetts held a state election which resulted in the election of the famous James Michael Curley to his one and only term as Governor. Nantucket ran true to form and voted heavily Republican, giving Curley only 442 votes. Curley responded in kind and rewarded the Island with the appointment of Miss Caroline Leveen as Justice of the District Court. Miss Leveen, a lawyer in the office of Boston attorney John Paul Feeney, was a shrewd businesswoman, a registered pharmacist, and a package-store proprietor. She came to Nantucket, purchased some real estate, and took over the District Court, where she reigned for thirty-three years.

Judge Leveen had no great difficulty in deciding criminal cases because, as she often reminded the defendants, "The police would not bring you in here unless you were guilty."

On the civil side, the rules were equally simple. "The Plaintiff must get some money out of this." Therefore, a trial before the justice was something of a set piece; she always presided in silence, never asking a question and never ruling on evidence. When the little drama was over, the judge found the defendant guilty and asked the chief of police what the fine should be. Occasionally, in misreading the complaint, the judge found the police officer guilty, and sometimes she found the witness guilty, but it was clear that *somebody* in the room was guilty. The fines were small, but the appeals were many, and for the litigant willing to take his case to a Superior Court jury, justice was eventually done.

In her court, it was not unusual for an attorney to lose a score of cases in a row. To win a case was a triumph. One day, in a masterpiece of sheer confusion, the great event happened. A local lawyer was defending a drunken driving case, and, having little else to say in defense, continually hammered at the argument, "but my client is a successful businessman!" After listening to hours of testimony without saying a word, and hearing the repetitive argument of the defense attorney, the judge ruled, "I find the defendant is a successful businessman," and walked off the bench. That was the closest she came to a "not guilty."

The Nantucket District Court was the scene of a startling legal confrontation in 1907. Nantucket's celebrated fight against the automobile began when the islanders seized upon the language of a 1905 law authorizing the Selectmen to ban automobiles from "particular streets and ways" of the Town. Acting under this law, and trying to preserve the peace and tranquillity of the Island streets, the Selectmen promptly banned automobiles from "all the highways on Nantucket." The Town was virtually unanimous in its opposition to cars, but three off-island car owners and a few summer residents of 'Sconset wanted the right to operate their vehicles on the Island. They soon found a ready champion in Boston attorney William A. Thibodeau, founder of and counsel for the Massachusetts Automobile Legal Association. After several wrangles with the Selectmen and hearings before the Massachusetts Highway Commission, Thibodeau conceived a plan to test the Nantucket regulation in the courts, and he found a unique method of leaping from the local District Court to the Supreme Judicial Court in Boston.

Thibodeau launched a task force of three Maxwell touring cars which rolled off Steamboat Wharf with the lead car driven by Frank J. Tyler, owner and president of the Maxwell-Briscoe Company of Boston. Sitting smugly in the back seat with his briefcase full of legal pleadings and bail money, was Attorney William A. Thibodeau. They chugged through the public streets, posed for the necessary photographs under the Selectmen's "Automobiles Excluded" sign, and awaited the arrival of the chief of police, who promptly handed Tyler his summons to the District Court.

For two days before the trial, Tyler ran his Maxwell around Nantucket on test rides and demonstrations. He gave the local *Inquirer and Mirror* an interview, stating, "I brought the car to the Island simply to make a test of the rule the Selectmen have made to exclude all automobiles from the Island. I did not come down to antagonize you. . . . If the law can be enforced, and the people of the Island want it, all well and good." The *Inquirer and Mirror* editorialized about the mechanized invaders, "The members of the party are all gentlemen, in the true sense of the word, and were treated as such wherever they went, notwithstanding they were automobilists."

The great confrontation in the Nantucket District Court, where Judge George E. Mooers presided, took place on August 30, 1907.[1]

When court convened, Judge Mooers first completed his arraignment of the defendant and then asked for his plea. Before Tyler could answer, Sheriff Josiah Barrett walked slowly down the center aisle of the courtroom and strode up to the bench. Speaking slowly and clearly, he said, "Your Honor, I have a summons."

"A summons?" the judge asked, "And from whom?"

"From the Supreme Judicial Court of Massachusetts."

"Who is it for?" asked the judge.

"It's for you, Your Honor," replied Sheriff Barrett solemnly.

Stunned silence fell over the courtroom. The crowd of spectators looked at each other in astonishment. Attorney Thibodeau smiled and gazed at the ceiling. The sheriff stood with arms folded. Finally, the silence was broken when a spectator turned and said, "My God—he's arrested the judge!"

Attorney Thibodeau had brought a Writ of Prohibition against Judge Mooers, demanding that His Honor appear before the Supreme Judicial Court in Boston to justify his prosecution of this defendant and threatening him with contempt for refusal to obey. Round one in the battle went to the motorists.

Judge Mooers obeyed his summons to Boston, where a hearing was held before Justice Caleb Loring, complete with witnesses, testimony, and the Nantucket judge in the dock. Mr. Justice Loring promptly ruled from the bench that the Writ of Prohibition was an extraordinary remedy not applicable to the case and dismissed it. Judge Mooers was returned to his bench. Showing admirable restraint under the circumstances, Judge Mooers found Tyler guilty of violating the Nantucket Auto Exclusion By-law and imposed a fine of $25. Round two was a victory for Nantucket.

Tyler claimed an appeal to the Superior Court. Judge Mooers imposed $200 cash bail, and Thibodeau produced it from his briefcase, thus freeing Tyler and his Maxwell for another day. In October 1907 the justice of the Superior Court ordered a

[1] Edouard A. Stackpole, "Nantucket versus the Chug-Buggy," *Automobile Quarterly*, Volume XV, No. 1, First Quarter, 1977.

directed verdict of "not guilty" for Tyler, ruling the Nantucket ordinance was too broad in its sweep; the Selectmen could legally exclude automobiles from "*particular* roads and ways," but not from "*all* the highways on Nantucket." Round three and the Battle of 1907 had been won by the auto.

Undaunted by their setback in court, the Nantucket Board of Selectmen convened the next day and issued new regulations which did, indeed, exclude automobiles from "particular roads and ways," to wit, every street which gave access to Steamboat Wharf and the other wharves of the Town, thus preventing any invasion by vehicles upon any known landing place. Short of an amphibious or airborne vehicle, Nantucket was secure. It remained secure through legislative battles, commission hearings, and Town Meeting referenda, until 1918, when a combination of pressures from the World War, summer residents, and the development of outlying lands resulted in Nantucket's repeal of its auto exclusion law. The first "legal" auto arrived on May 16, and it was a Maxwell.

Any tale of Nantucket litigants must include the saga of Clinton S. Folger, the man who dragged Nantucket into the automobile age with his famous "horsemobile." Actually, it was a 1913 Overland and it was destined to become Nantucket's most notorious motor vehicle. During the years from 1908 to 1912, Nantucket operated under a local option law which permitted the Selectmen to exclude autos from "certain streets and ways" of the Town, and the populace supported this regulation with few exceptions. The one road the Selectmen could not control was the six-mile State Highway from the First Milestone to the village of 'Sconset, which was beyond their jurisdiction. Clint Folger was a liveryman of highly independent character, and he had the contract to carry the U. S. Mail from the steamboat to the post office in 'Sconset. He also had a peculiar notion that he had a right to operate an automobile. The Town thought otherwise, and one week after the infamous Overland arrived on the Island in November, 1913, a Town Meeting was held in which the largest number of voters in a century appeared and voted overwhelmingly against the operation of any vehicles within the limits of the Town.

Clint Folger decided the mail must go through to 'Sconset,

so he continued to operate his Overland through the Town streets, where he was apprehended, dragged into the District Court, and fined $15, a judgment he appealed. The law was being challenged, but it was one man against the Town, and Folger was running out of money for fines and bail. It was then he conceived his master plan for a campaign against the auto exclusion law.

On December 19, the townsfolk were startled to see Clint Folger set out from his stable with the Overland running at one horsepower: hitched to the front of the vehicle was his patient and sturdy horse. The reins ran back over the windshield and through the steering wheel to Folger's hands. At the start of the State Highway, near the First Milestone, the horse was unhitched and pastured to graze on the Lewis Farm pasture, while Clint Folger cranked up the Overland and set sail to 'Sconset. When he returned from his rounds, the horse was hitched back to the car and they returned in triumph to the stable.

Clint Folger continued his one-man campaign on behalf of the automobile for several years. So long as he adhered to the "horsemobile" arrangement, the Town had no cause to complain; but when he turned defiant and dispensed with the horse, he was again arrested and fined, this time $60. He became a leader in the growing campaign to repeal the Nantucket law, until finally in 1918, while his last appeal was still pending, the Town succumbed to the pressures of the modern age and voted, 336 to 296, to allow motor vehicles to be operated on the Island.

The semiannual sessions of the Superior Court in Nantucket were special occasions for the Island Bar. They were marked by a combination of dignity and camaraderie which spoke well for the court and the Island. In the early days, the presiding judge, riding the Superior Court circuit, usually came to Nantucket for one week, then traveled to Martha's Vineyard for the following week. With a light docket and good weather on his side, the judge often brought his wife along for the week; otherwise, the local attorneys usually arranged some social life to welcome the visiting jurist. The sheriff would meet the Sunday boat and escort the judge to his quarters, which were usually at the Roberts House in the old days.

With a little advance notice to the Roberts sisters, the judge would be lodged in the "Governor's Room," where Governor Charles Hurley stayed during his visits, and, although the hostel had no public bar, it was not unusual to find a bottle or two provided by the management.

The opening of the court was always preceded by great activity, with sheriffs, lawyers, and the clerk of courts arriving early for the last-minute preparations. The jury members usually arrived early, dressed in their best, and always asking how soon they could get back to work. When the roll call revealed a missing juror, the deputies were sent scurrying to round him up, and he was brought before the judge, overalls and all, to apologize for his forgetfulness. It was also a time for reunion among the lawyers, with the District Attorney and his assistants from the mainland greeting the Island lawyers and renewing old acquaintances.

Before the construction of the present court house in 1965, the Superior Court sessions were held almost anywhere; in Bennett Hall, Cyrus Pierce School, or in various private social halls and meeting rooms. The facilities left much to be desired by modern standards, but many visitors remembered the experience with a touch of nostalgia. Most of the judges were able to rule on legal questions without benefit of the law books, quoting by memory rather accurately from the rulings of the Supreme Judicial Court.

The atmosphere of the Nantucket sessions of the Superior Court may have been one of informality, but the quality of justice dispensed was often the highest. Because the judge sitting in Nantucket was faced with few major criminal cases, the semiannual sessions were something of a respite from the heavy criminal dockets found in the city courts, and, therefore, the trip to Nantucket was considered a reward for the veteran judges of the Superior Court. One of the most colorful and independent members of the Massachusetts judiciary was Judge Frank J. Donahue, who was the Senior Justice of the Superior Court when he came to Nantucket in the 1960s. His reputation for meting out stern justice and long sentences caused fear and trembling among the defendants and their lawyers. The court session that year had a long list of drug cases, the first on the Island, the result of a State Police raid which had netted a score of young people housed in various crash pads throughout the Town. Massachusetts then had a law making it a crime to be "present where marijuana is found," which carried a penalty of two and one-half years in jail. Under this law, everyone in the houses was arrested, and most were quickly convicted. The prospect of defending the cases before this judge was a dismal one, and, since the local juries had little sympathy to offer the defendants, it looked like the cases could not be won without an appeal to the Supreme Judicial Court.

One of the authors represented a twenty-year-old lad who was the son of a wealthy New Yorker in the publishing business. The defendant was found asleep in a three-room cottage, which the police described as "chock full of junk," and the troopers found a stash of marijuana under his bed. He faced a jail sentence, and this judge was certain to oblige him. We spent the days before the trial preparing a number of lengthy motions and an elaborate brief attacking the law, the facts and the situation. The final draft of the brief took most of the night, but was finally ready on the morning of the trial.

On the morning of the trial, as Judge Donahue ordered his breakfast of porridge, bacon, and eggs at the Jared Coffin House where he was staying, he spotted across the dining room Assistant District Attorney Joseph P. Harrington of New Bedford, who had arrived to prosecute the case. The judge asked Harrington what was on the docket for the day, and was told that it was a case involving the charge of being present where marijuana was found. The judge spluttered into his porridge and said, "Unconstitutional, absolutely unconstitutional! That law cannot be upheld. Why, if that law were valid, everybody in this hotel, or everybody in the courtroom could be found guilty!" The trial that morning lasted ten minutes, the defendant was found "not guilty," and the judge repeated his reasoning to a crowded courtroom. A few years later, Judge Donahue was vindicated when the Supreme Judicial Court held that the law, as we first learned in Nantucket, was unconstitutional.

Judge Donahue usually displayed his common sense and independence most notably when giving his brief, but colorful instructions to the jury. One day he presided at the trial of a local youth charged with drunkenness and driving under the influence.

When the jury returned and asked for the legal definition of drunkenness, the judge intoned:

> Not drunk is he who from the floor,
> Can rise and have just one drink more.
> But drunk is he who prostrate lies,
> And who can neither drink nor rise.

The court session came only twice a year, but court business was handled year-round by the clerk. Wesley Fordyce held this position for thirty-two years, during which he often displayed a streak of independence which startled visiting judges. On one occasion, while filling in for the District Court Clerk, he was confronted with an irate husband who claimed his wife had run away with another man. So the clerk promptly issued the husband a search warrant to find his wife and bring her home. On the eve of his retirement, Clerk Fordyce was assigned to a jury session presided over by a short-tempered jurist noted for his courtroom tirades. While one jury case was on trial, the judge decided to speed up the proceedings and ordered the clerk to impanel the next jury. The clerk became fuddled and reached in the wrong box, starting to call out the names of the jurors who were already hearing the first case. When the judge snapped at him, Clerk Fordyce retorted, "Things would go a lot better around here if you tried only one case at a time." The judge bellowed, "I will try all the cases I want! And you, Mr. Clerk, had better apologize to the court or you will find yourself a defendant in your own courtroom!" The spectators sat in stunned silence, expecting to see the seventy-five-year-old clerk dragged away in chains to spend his retirement in the clink. After many minutes, which seemed like hours, Fordyce turned to the judge and apologized. Both clerk and judge retired within the year, but, following the great tradition of those early Nantucket Court clerks, Peter Folger and Benjamin Gardner, Wesley Fordyce will always be remembered for the final hour of his long career.

Probate Judge George M. Poland, who practiced law in Nantucket until his death at the age of ninety-six was often called upon for criminal cases which he handled with great ability. In addition, his knowledge of ancient land law made him a busy practitioner in the field of real estate controversies and Land Court cases. Once he was called to try a complicated real estate case before a jury at Edgartown on Martha's Vineyard. His opponent was State Senator William A. Morse, from the Vineyard, who was famed as the greatest persuader of juries ever to practice on that island. When it came to the final arguments, both lawyers reached for their best strategies. Judge Poland, always the gentleman, began by apologizing to the worthy citizens on the jury for "daring to appear on their island in opposition to their noted Senator, who was famed across the Commonwealth for his ability to sway the Vineyard juries." While admitting that he himself knew a little bit about real estate law, Judge Poland claimed that he was unskilled in oratory and unlikely to convince the jury in the face of such a formidable foe. The Senator then argued more successfully. True, he admitted, he had some success in the past appearing before juries in routine matters of the law where mere words might make a difference, but he knew little of the complexities of these ancient land titles, whereas his opponent was an acknowledged expert on the subject. "In fact," he proclaimed, "it is said of Judge Poland that on his home Island of Nantucket, he is capable of grasping a single grain of sand blowing in the wind, and trace its record title back to the first Indian inhabitant of Nantucket." Morse won the case.

Nantucket Probate Court Judge Jeremiah J. Sullivan was one of the best-liked jurists in the state, and was noted for his expeditious handling of cases, no matter how unusual or complicated they might appear. On one occasion, he was presented a novel problem resulting from the disappearance of an airplane off Nantucket, but he solved the mystery with judicial dispatch and the aid of a dramatic item of evidence.

During the summer of 1973 a summer resident took off from New Jersey in his private plane for a weekend with his family in Nantucket. He was an experienced pilot who had made the trip many times before, and his flight was routinely tracked up the coast by the various control stations until he made his final approach to the shore of the Island in the early evening. Then the plane suddenly vanished from the radar screen and was never seen again. An air and sea search failed to find any trace of the plane or pilot.

The mysterious disappearance presented not only a personal tragedy but a legal dilemma, for his property and business affairs could not be managed until his estate was administered. Although Massachusetts will permit an estate to be probated based upon a petition under oath reciting the fact of death, it will not issue a death certificate until the body is found and identified, while the law of New Jersey required some proof of death before the estate could be probated. Faced with this dilemma, the New Jersey family decided to file a petition in the Nantucket Probate Court, reciting the facts and requesting the Nantucket Town Clerk to file a certificate establishing the ultimate conclusion of the pilot's death.

When the case came on for a hearing before Judge Sullivan, the petitioner produced evidence of the plane's flight plan, the records of the FAA's last contact with the plane, a private investigation of the disappearance, and the fruitless search for the plane. Although the judge was sympathetic, he waited impatiently for some hard evidence that the plane had in fact crashed in Nantucket waters. It arrived from an unlikely source when the court-house janitor, Henry Garnett, an amateur beachcomber, entered the courtroom rolling an airplane tire he had found on the beach near the airport. As the tire rolled toward the bench, Judge Sullivan barked, "That's good enough for me!" He quickly signed the legal order and brought the case to a speedy and satisfactory conclusion.

16
Law and Order

The enforcing of the criminal law is difficult in any community, but on Nantucket it has always posed some unusual problems. Maintaining the public peace on an island where everyone is more or less confined as upon a ship would appear to be an easy task, and to the casual summer visitor the Island seems so peaceful and enjoyable that the very thought of law enforcement seems alien to the atmosphere. In the early years of the settlement, the Town got by with only a fire watch to patrol the streets at night and a rudimentary establishment of deputies and constables to handle any strangers who violated the tranquillity of the Town. As an island, Nantucket had no difficulty in identifying strangers to the community and found it expedient to resort to that most favored of all punishments, banishment:

"The sentence of the Court is that Edward Cowles shall be soundly whipt, and to go away from the island on the same vessall that he came in. And when he is aboard the vessall he is not to come a shore upon the penalty of being whipt every time that he come a shore."

The Yankee frugality of the inhabitants was most evident in the Town's indifference to its court house and jail facilities. In the benign hope that such accommodations would seldom be needed on the Island, Nantucket adopted a tradition of making do without formal dedication of any permanent court house, preferring to use any available space on a temporary basis. The earliest records indicate the only wrongdoers were the hapless Indians, usually stimulated by the white man's rum, for which they were quickly and informally punished with whippings or a stretch in the stocks. Most of the settlers followed the Quaker tradition of brotherly love, which maintained the peace by mutual consent. Once Nantucket gained its prominence as a maritime center, the Island felt the impact of hundreds of sailors from every port in the world, and the Town was finally forced to build a jail in 1696 for the accommodation of rowdy sailors. This jail, claimed to be the first prison in the country, was built by William Bunker, who agreed to maintain it for a year at a fee of "four pounds, half in wheat, the other in graine." This establishment was eventually replaced by the famous Old Jail, built on Vestal Street in 1805 and still maintained as a historical monument. The Old Jail was seldom used and was regularly condemned by both citizens and inmates alike. The only prisoner in the jail in 1870 wrote the Selectmen bitterly that, if they did not fix up the jail so the sheep couldn't get in and bother him, he'd be damned if he would stay there any longer. Nevertheless, it remained in use for many years.

On October 3, 1932, the last inmate of the Old Nantucket Jail escaped and was smuggled off the Island. Charles Freeman, a young black man who lived in Codfish Park, had been apprehended in New Bedford and was brought to the Island to await action by the Grand Jury on a charge of sodomy. Early one evening, he called to the jailer, Edgar Ellis, who lived next to the jail, crying that he needed a drink of water. When the elderly attendant arrived, Freeman slugged him with a chunk of masonry ripped from the cell floor, left Ellis dazed and bleeding, and escaped down Vestal Street.

The Island was shocked by the violent act and alarmed at the thought of a dangerous fugitive on the loose. "How could any man escape from the Nantucket Jail?" everyone asked, for no prisoner had ever escaped in the past 217 years. "He'll never get off the Island!" But he did.

The police called out a large posse: American Legion reserves and unemployed volunteers swept the Island for several days. They were aided by State Police under Sergeant Harvey Laprade who brought "a stalwart bunch of well-trained huskies," to the Island, and a search plane. The State Police brought with them the first dog trained to track men ever seen on Nantucket—a German shepherd named Tzep, who took orders only in German, but could not find Freeman in any language. In those days, the only way off the Island was the daily steamboat, but Freeman disappeared, allegedly aided by friends who smuggled him aboard the boat in a laundry basket.

Two years after the escape, the *Inquirer and Mirror* noted that he was still missing, but reported that the islanders felt safer knowing Freeman was off-island than they would if he were locked up in the Nantucket Jail.

Charles Freeman was eventually recaptured because of a bizarre chain of circumstances which could occur only on Nantucket. In 1937, Ray Morris, the Town Tax Collector, advertised a tax-taking of several properties on the Island, including the home of Mary Freeman, mother of Charles. Ever vigilant to protect his Nantucket homestead, but not overly intelligent, Freeman wrote a letter to Ray Morris from California seeking to redeem the property. The Tax Collector promptly handed the letter to his friend, Police Chief Mooney, who made one telephone call. Soon the California Police were knocking on Freeman's door.

At the July 1938 session of the Nantucket Superior Court, Judge Francis J. Good sentenced Charles Freeman, who had waived counsel and a jury trial. The judge handed him five years for the escape, five years for the assault of Jailer Ellis, and twelve to fifteen years for sodomy, to be served concurrently. Freeman went to Charlestown State Prison, and his house was sold for unpaid taxes.

During the early years of the 1880s, Nantucket was experiencing the first stirrings of its popularity as a summer resort and meeting the first of the new leisure class. For years, the Island had struggled to escape the doldrums and depression which had enveloped the community since the decline of the whaling fleet and the collapse of the local economy. Inspired by a realization of the value of the Island climate and location, and encouraged by a few local boosters, Nantucket sought to establish itself as a modern summer resort. Both Island businessmen and off-island speculators joined in the effort to promote Nantucket among the prospective East Coast clientele, and the vacation business seemed to promise the salvation of the Island. The wildest dreams seemed to have possibilities and almost any venture could command financial support. Most of the speculations were dismal failures. Some of the proposed construction and land development was openly ballyhooed, while other projects were shrouded in mystery and intrigue.

One unusual piece of construction took place at remote Squam Head, overlooking the broad expanse of the Atlantic from the easternmost limit of the Island. An elaborate and expensive estate was constructed, complete with a large brick stable, using bricks from a recently demolished bank on Main Street.

The Island hummed with rumors about the purpose of this suspicious and elegant enterprise: it was going to be a summer hotel; it was to be a country club for the very rich; worst of all, it was to be a gambling casino for wealthy sportsmen and their fancy ladies. Other stories were quickly spread about plans to construct wharves and piers to berth the yachts of wealthy visitors from New York and Newport, plans which defied all local knowledge of the tides and shoals. Nantucket was intensely concerned and curious.

The concern was increased when it was revealed that the man behind the project was William H. Chadwick, the cashier of the Pacific National Bank of Nantucket. The bank was the depository of most of the Island's money. Mr. Chadwick was a solid businessman with a reputation for integrity who had been very active in local real estate operations. Because of his standing in the community, he was never considered the principal behind the Squam Head construction, but was reputed to be the agent for "parties abroad." In any event, it was Chadwick who bore the brunt of the subsequent events and lent his name to the ill-fated building.

In early 1885, it was discovered that William H. Chadwick had been building his dream house in part with funds of the Pacific National Bank. A bank examiner discovered he had falsified entries and had withdrawn $11,500 from the bank by various means. He had also borrowed heavily from people in Nantucket, amassing a total debt of about $50,000, a huge sum in those days.

The Town's reaction was one of stunned disbelief. Chadwick

immediately lost his position at the bank, and the real estate venture collapsed with him. His father stepped forward and paid off his bank debt in full, and his other local debts were settled by various means. Humiliated but never convicted, Chadwick lived to see his magnificent Squam property auctioned off in 1894.

The big house known as Chadwick's Folly remained for many years on the bluff at Squam Head, but subsequent owners gradually dismantled it for summer cottages, and only the brooding empty derelict shell of the mansion remained. In time the house was cut up into separate cottages, the huge cupola alone proving sufficient for a small shack. The last remains were leveled in 1956.

The case never went to court, and Chadwick would never discuss the subject. Rumors held that he was duped by his friends on the mainland, who withdrew their promised support and left him to bear the financial and personal burden of their commercial dream. Who was behind it all, and why the respected banker succumbed to the scheme has never been told, and probably never will.

The Town of Nantucket was always noted for its municipal thrift, and the upkeep of a police force, like the courts, was considered a matter of bare necessity. The chief and officers of the Police Department were appointed annually by the Selectmen in the days before Civil Service, and when times were hard and jobs were scarce, the police were considered fortunate to have regular paychecks, however small. The Town was also fortunate to have the services of several able and conscientious men, who, without formal training, relied on their common sense and knowledge of the Island to keep the peace, and occasionally, perform impressive feats of detective work.

One of these able men was Houghton Gibbs, a tall, dignified man who served as chief of police from 1913 to 1934. Chief Gibbs investigated a break-in at Frank Holdgate's store in 'Sconset in 1922 and solved one of Nantucket's most unusual crimes with a brilliant piece of criminal identification, and only one clue to work on. The chief learned that the criminal had made the mistake of leaving one item of evidence at the scene of the crime. It happened to be his nose, which the chief scooped from the floor of the robbery scene. Since Nantucket had very few suspects without noses, the chief did not need the FBI to tell him where to look. Carrying the delicate evidence in his hand, the chief strode down the Gully Road into Codfish Park, where he knocked on the door of Walter Kelly, a black gentleman who had Ben Turpin eyes and no nose whatsoever; or rather, two noses. It seems that Kelly first came to Nantucket in answer to an advertisement from a movie producer for an extraordinarily homely man to play a role as a pirate in an early film. Kelly was not only elected for this starring role on sight, but made enough money to buy himself two false noses: one for weekdays and one for Sundays. When Chief Gibbs, carrying the weekday nose, knocked on his door, Walter Kelly answered the door wearing his Sunday nose, and the Chief needed only to produce a calendar to prove his case.

When Chief Gibbs died in 1934, he was succeeded by Lawrence F. Mooney. Born on a farm in Polpis, Chief Mooney never received any formal police training, but possessed the most important qualifications for a small-town policeman: common sense and good humor. His brother, Robert C. Mooney, left Nantucket as a young man to become a highly respected detective with the Boston Police Department. Chief Mooney remained on the Island to serve thirty-nine years with the Nantucket Police Department, where he was best known for his natural ability for dealing with the public and his good-natured manner of handling local problems.

Each summer the local police force was augmented by a number of special officers appointed to manage the seasonal influx of summer tourists. One year a local youth from 'Sconset was appointed to patrol that sleepy village, seven miles from Town. Chief Mooney called him into the station, gave him his instructions, and handed him his badge, belt and service revolver. The next day the young man returned and asked him for more ammunition. Peering suspiciously over his glasses, the chief asked him what had become of the six bullets he had received with the gun, and the officer innocently replied he had used them all on target practice. The chief shook his head wearily, reached into the lower drawer of his desk and slowly counted out six more slugs. Handing them to the officer, he said, "Here is your ammunition, and I want every damn one back after Labor Day!"

The temporary officers were always a source of some amusement as they struggled to master their new responsibilities. One day a summer officer stopped a car in 'Sconset and demanded to see the driver's license, from which he learned the driver lived in Philadelphia. "All right, mister," said the officer suspiciously, "now tell me how come your car has Pennsylvania license plates?" When the judicial revolution of the recent years made the police aware of the Miranda warnings, another temporary officer found a neat way of taking care of all constitutional questions by testifying in court, "I immediately apprehended the defendant, and the very first thing I did was warn him about the Constitution."

Lest the reader gather the lawyers always outwitted the local police in the courtroom, one of the authors remembers a drunken driving case when the police had the last laugh. A gay little pioneer of the local artists' colony came wheeling home early on January 1 from a lively New Year's Eve party. Bubbling over with high spirits and New Year's resolutions, he wove his way home through the narrow streets, nicking a few parked cars along the way. When an officer in a police cruiser waved him to pull over, he waved back and sang out, "It's all right, fellas, I'm almost home!" He did not make it; the police cruiser stopped him and he was put under arrest. The whole incident was most unfortunate, he told his lawyer before the trial, because he knew the handsome young officer who arrested him would never have done so but for the presence of another policeman riding with him, a mean, swarthy fellow with a nasty disposition.

When the trial was held before Judge George Anastos, the little defendant testified eloquently about that other policeman who sat silently sneering at him behind his heavy beard that evening. No, he could not identify him because they were both wearing heavy trooper caps with "those fuzzy earmuffs," but he did not see him in the courtroom. Flushed with triumph, the defense attorney sat down, ready to argue that the missing policeman was an essential witness who should have been produced in court. At this point, the young officer returned to the stand and was asked, "Who was with you in the cruiser?"

He calmly answered, "I was alone—except for the police dog sitting beside me."

The game defendant leaned over to his lawyer and muttered, "I told you he needed a shave!"

Wendell H. Howes, who started his career on the Nantucket Police Department as a rookie patrolman in 1936, became chief of police in 1952, and retired in 1975 after thirty-nine years of service to the Town. He survived many years of change and controversy which saw the Town grow from a sleepy summer resort to a bustling year-round community whose problems increased each year. For many years he was Nantucket's most familiar figure on Main Street, where he observed the Town scene from his favorite spot in front of the Pacific Club. He applied his own brand of common sense and law enforcement to the Island's problems with remarkable success. At the time when Massachusetts had a law forbidding "idle and disorderly persons," the local police were known to intercept the unwashed and the unwanted on Steamboat Wharf and turn them around if they had no money, job, or purpose for being in Town. This early "Anti-Hippie Law" was later held to be unconstitutional, much to the Chief's regret, but he always had the support of the Town.

In 1961 Massachusetts faced a dramatic confrontation over enforcement of the Sunday "Blue Laws," which prohibited any type of retail business from being conducted on the Lord's Day. These laws, a holdover from the Puritan days, were strongly supported by the Irish and Catholic majority which governed the state, but were particularly irritating to a summer resort which needed to maximize its business opportunities during a short summer season. When questioned by the press, the chief announced that he thought the laws were silly and he would not enforce them in Nantucket. The issue erupted when Governor John A. Volpe and Attorney General Edward J. McCormack decreed that the laws must be enforced and called upon the chief to resign if he did not do his duty. Howes did not resign, and his stand gained him widespread approval on the Island. Chief Howes gained a great deal of personal satisfaction years later when Governor Michael Dukakis recommended abolition of the Blue Laws as detrimental to the state's economy. Meanwhile, in Nantucket, business was better than ever.

In the summer of 1964, a legal mishap and the local reaction produced a public wrangle of spectacular proportions. The Island

Service Company owned the South Wharf where an excursion vessel from Hyannis carrying as many as 300 passengers landed daily. Differences developed between Walter Beinecke, Jr., who controlled Island Service Company, and Ted Gelinas, who owned and operated the Hyannis boat. The situation came to a head on a hot August 1, when Gelinas' lease expired and Beinecke decreed he must sign a new lease before the boat could land, although the terms of the lease were in dispute. Word reached the Island that with or without a lease, the Hyannis boat was under way and headed for Nantucket. The Beinecke forces deployed to meet the invasion. The Island Service manager, Bud Egan, ordered dozens of the company's truck drivers, laborers, and handymen to prepare to repel boarders, while crowds gathered to watch the promised spectacle.

Promply at high noon, the M.V. *Martha's Vineyard* with Captain Ted Gelinas at the helm, steamed into the harbor, carrying 300 hot and expectant tourists ready to view the fabled sights of peaceful Nantucket. Equally expectant, dozens of Nantucketers, following their boss's orders, ringed the dock with stern determination. The vessel's crew threw the lines ashore—and the sturdy defenders threw them back. The gangplank was pushed across and provoked a wrestling match on the wharf. Captain Gelinas leaped ashore yelling to his crew and was wrestled to the ground. The entire crew of the *Martha's Vineyard* swarmed ashore, carrying the modern equivalent of belaying pins, to meet the Island Service men in pitched battle. In the confusion, somebody got a line over. The hapless vessel was moored to the dock, her 300 passengers lining the rail to stare at the brawl.

Most of the passengers on the boat were tourists seeing Nantucket for the first time. They had heard of the Island's reputation for quaintness and charm, but nothing had prepared them for this. The wharf was now the scene of a violent melee, with men wrestling, shouting and throwing punches. The captain was hog-tied, the crew was being pummeled, and local youths were running to join the fun. As visitors in a strange land, the passengers trembled and wondered what lay ahead of them if they dared venture ashore. Finally, one man on the ship called to a bystander on the dock, "What's going on here? Is Nantucket always like this?"

The native wit drawled out a casual reply, "Hell, mister, this ain't nothing—wait till you see what's happening on Main Street!"

Finally, the chief of police arrived, separated the contestants, listened to their stories, and pronounced this a civil dispute to be settled by lawyers. Everyone agreed it was important to get the passengers ashore and help stimulate the Island economy. When this was done, everyone dusted himself off and went back to work.

Captain Gelinas claimed to have injured his shoulder in the brawl, for which he brought an action for damages in Barnstable Superior Court. For the lawyers defending the Island Service Company and its employees, the trial proved to be a good lesson in the fallibility of human memory, because each man emphatically denied laying hands on anyone. As the trial proceeded, it was realized most of the 300 passengers had been carrying cameras, for the Gelinas attorneys produced dozens of action photographs, and even promised movies of the debacle. Many of the pictures would have surpassed Hollywood for violence in action, with every punch and wrestling grip vividly portrayed. One of our "innocent bystanders," shown a three-foot enlargement of his stranglehold on the captain, was forced to admit he had been "sort of acting as a peacemaker, just trying to calm him down." Eventually the battery of defense lawyers agreed that discretion was the better part of valor and the Battle of the Beachhead was ended with a substantial cash settlement.

Because Nantucket had few serious criminal cases for many years, the local police usually prosecuted their own cases in the District Court. Beginning in 1970, the increasing complexity of the criminal law and the appearance of appointed defense counsel required by the *Gideon* decision brought about the appointment of the first professional Town Prosecutor. One of the local lawyers was appointed to the task of prosecuting all the Island's criminals. The office of the Town District Attorney helped restore the balance between prosecution and defense in criminal trials, and the wheels of justice seemed to roll more smoothly. It also provided one of the authors with a brief moment in the limelight during Nantucket's most publicized trial of recent memory.

In August 1973, Joseph P. Kennedy, III, son of the late Senator Robert F. Kennedy, was driving an open jeep which overturned on Polpis Road, spilling seven passengers and causing permanent injuries to eighteen-year-old Pamela Kelley. The accident took place in mid-afternoon while the young people were touring the Island, and the investigation revealed no drugs or alcohol involved. Nantucket police investigated and brought charges against twenty-year-old Kennedy for driving negligently so as to endanger the lives and safety of the public.

There is no more certain method in America of arousing the interest of the press and public than to have a famous name connected with a criminal trial. Although the case was a routine matter for the police and the court, the name of the defendant soon turned it into a cause célèbre. The Island swarmed with reporters who bombarded prosecution and defense with demands for information from all sides. The courtroom was crowded with members of the national press as well as five London reporters; the building was ringed with television crews and cameras, and a crowd of 600 spectators. Under such circumstances, every rumor from Nantucket became national news, and the dividing line between the rights of fair trial and free press was often strained.

In addition to the notoriety of the Kennedy name, the accident was subject to comparison with the Chappaquiddick tragedy of 1969, which had taken place only 20 miles away on neighboring Martha's Vineyard. With every move of the police, prosecution and defense subject to the closest scrutiny, everyone was determined to avoid repetition of the mistakes which had turned the earlier accident into a national controversy.

From the Kennedy compound in Hyannis, the members of the family and their attorneys conducted themselves with dignity and integrity throughout their latest ordeal. They retained Nantucket Attorney Wayne Holmes. Their most immediate concern was the fate of family friend Pamela Kelley, who hovered between life and death, but eventually recovered, disabled for life. Had she not survived, the charge against Kennedy would have been manslaughter.

In the days before the trial, the pressure seemed to mount steadily on Nantucket and it reached some strange limits. Once word of the Kennedy accident hit the press, the local Volkswagen dealer received a telephone call from Volkswagen of America, anxious to know whether one of its vehicles had been involved. The battered jeep, which happened to be a Toyota, had been towed to an Island garage, but was besieged by so many investigators and reporters that the police had to hide it in 'Sconset for security purposes. The Town Prosecutor began to receive the first hate mail of his career, all bitterly anti-Kennedy. The police chief refused to talk to anybody. The carefree pace of August in Nantucket had been rudely interrupted, and by a routine accident. But, as columnist George Frazier wrote, anything a Kennedy does is important because he or she is a Kennedy.

A week after the accident, the case came to trial before Judge George Anastos. The trial itself was no different from many others; the testimony was routine, the lawyers performed their roles and the spectators listened closely to testimony without hearing anything sensational. But there was a difference that day, for in the first row of seats sat Joseph P. Kennedy, III, his mother, Ethel Kennedy, and his uncle, Senator Edward M. Kennedy. Reporters scribbled furiously while courtroom artists sketched the scene. Veteran columnist George Frazier decided he could get a better story outside the building, so he spent the morning interviewing the crowd gathered on the sidewalk, including one young woman who had camped on the front steps of the court house at 5:30 A.M. to be sure of a seat at the trial.

After all the witnesses, the diagrams, the pictures, and the arguments, it was up to the judge. The courtroom was silent when he spoke.

First, he found Kennedy guilty, and, then with the defendant standing before him, said, "I realize I am sitting in judgment on the son of Robert F. Kennedy, a man whom I knew and admired, although we did not always agree on various matters. I was a classmate of your uncle, for whom you are named. You had a fine father and you have a fine mother. You carry an illustrious name, and I hope you will use that name for doing good and set an example for other young people, rather than appearing before me in a courtroom such as this."

The judge then added that he would treat this case as any other and imposed a $100 fine as recommended by the prosecutor. The case was over, and the principals departed, with Senator

Kennedy stopping to shake hands and say, "You were very fair." The media people rushed away with their stories and pictures, leaving quiet on the Island once more.

A flood of hate mail began to pour in to the judge and the prosecutor. Many of these crudely written messages came from distant states, but all contained bitter accusations against the defendant, his family, and Massachusetts justice. The most temperate of these letters simply read, "How much did the Kennedys pay you for this one?", while others revealed some twisted minds. We learned a solemn lesson about the burden of bearing a famous name.

17

The People's Choice

When the afternoon session of the Massachusetts House of Representatives was called to order, Speaker of the House Christian Herter stared in amazement at the solitary, white-haired representative who stood to be recognized for his maiden speech.

"The Chair recognizes the gentleman from Nantucket!"

The other members of the House were startled by the announcement, for Representative Orison V. Hull was a man of few words who had never spoken on the floor during his years in the House. He had served Nantucket as Selectman, fire chief, and police chief before being elected Representative at the age of seventy. In the House, he was noted for his silence and punctuality since he always arrived at the start of the 1:00 P.M. session and left at 4:00 P.M., which was his quitting time in Nantucket. His colleagues gazed in wonder as the Island's elder statesman marched solemnly toward the microphone where he bluntly pronounced,

"Mr. Speaker, last week I loaned my Red Sox pass to one of the members. I have forgotten which one. I would like it back."

He then sat down to thunderous applause and resumed his silent survey of the political scene.

The Island of Nantucket is a politically unique entity, being a town, county, and island all in one. It is the smallest county in Massachusetts and one of the smallest towns, governed by a five-person Board of Selectmen who also serve as County Commissioners. Until 1978, its sole delegate to the Commonwealth of

Massachusetts was one representative in the State Legislature, who was always the subject of much interest and occasional amusement in the State House due to his singular Island constituency and geographical situation.

The most colorful character the Island sent to Boston was the talented Micajah Coffin, "the anointed of the Island," who built a successful business as a merchant and mariner, then turned to politics and was elected Nantucket's representative for twenty-one years. Micajah had been educated in the classics at a private school run by his father, Benjamin, and his command of Latin combined with his natural speaking ability to make him a notable figure in the legislative body. In 1795 he promoted the legislative act which changed the name of the Town from Sherburne to Nantucket, a popular move and a practical necessity since Massachusetts already had a town in Middlesex County named Sherborn. His service in the legislature began under Massachusetts' first Governor, John Hancock, and continued under Samuel Adams, with the Town returning Coffin again and again until he reached the age of eighty, when he was succeeded by his eldest son, Gilbert. In his retirement he continued to be honored by his home town and greatly respected for his public service. When the day came in 1825 for the first gubernatorial visit to Nantucket, Governor Levi Lincoln marched up to Micajah Coffin's house on Pine Street and commended him for his long life of service to Town and state. Rising to the occasion, Micajah delivered a lengthy oration in classical Latin, while the Governor stared in amazement at this venerable Nantucketer, ninety-two years of age.

None of Micajah's successors was endowed with his many talents, but several went on to higher office. At one time the Town had three representatives in the legislature and Nantucketers were elected state senators, councillors, and congressmen, but the Island never produced a Governor. As the population dwindled during the nineteenth century, the importance of the sole representative in the State House declined accordingly.

Nantucket always had its favorite officeholders who usually ran without opposition and were returned to office year after year by the voters. Lauriston Bunker combined forty-five years as

Town Clerk with forty-three years as Register of Deeds, seldom missing a day on either job and never missing a Town Meeting. His successor, Charles Clark Coffin, performed the many functions of Town Clerk for thirty-five years, meeting the demands of amorous couples who insisted on his undertaking such occupational hazards as performing marriages on Altar Rock, several windy beaches, and one open boat. The Town usually showed its preference for the proven over the unknown, the common man over the professional, and the familiar Island name over the stranger. John J. Gardner, II, served the Town for fifty years as Register of Probate and Town Assessor—a record that has yet to be equaled—and showed his knowledge of the Island's voters when he rendered the following opinion after one election: "In this Town, a Barrett, a Holdgate, and a pair of overalls are always good for 500 votes."

The long terms of the Town officials were often attributed more to their consideration of their constituents than to their expertise in office. When Joseph Burgess was Superintendent of Schools in the 1930s he had a firm rule that any child entering the first grade must be born before January 1 of the proper year, and no exceptions could be made. One mother brought her youngster to school and insisted the boy was born in December and eligible for school, but his birth certificate showed he was born several months later, and was therefore too young. The mother said the birth certificate didn't matter, she knew when he was born and the official record was wrong. Mr. Burgess became curious about the situation, and went down to the Town Clerk's office to check it out with Lauriston Bunker. Old Mr. Bunker nodded wisely and said, "Oh, yes, I remember that one; she was a nice local girl who got into trouble, so I just moved up the birth certificate to nine months after the marriage. That boy is old enough to go to school."

A memorable commentary on the preoccupation of the local citizens was recorded for posterity by the Town Nurse, Miss Clementine Platt, in the Town Report of 1930. Nantucket was then suffering from the Depression and unemployment was widespread, leaving many husbands hanging around the house with nothing to do. The result should have been foreseen. Miss Platt felt it her duty to inform the Town: "There has been an increase of maternity work, doubtless due to unemployment at this time."

In years past, there were occasional civic-minded citizens who were neither elected nor appointed officeholders, but who perceived a public need and proceeded to fill it. Since many of the menfolk were absent at sea for long periods of time, hundreds of Nantucket women were left to keep their lonely vigils in empty houses. Although the Island women were famous for their self-reliance, their spirits often sagged during the long winters when howling northeast storms swept the Island, and all those lonely women in their drafty houses presented a community problem of some magnitude. A willing volunteer stepped forward with a ready solution; Benny Cleveland advertised that he was available to "sleep at the home of timid ladies for fifteen cents a night, or two nights for a quarter." His Yankee ingenuity produced a civic program which gained overwhelming acceptance. So highly regarded was Benny Cleveland that many suggested he should raise his rates, but he always declined for fear of losing some of his regular customers. Exhausted by his labors, the great man finally went to his reward in 1906, immortalized by "Benny Cleveland's Job."

When portents are abroad at night and tempests lash the shore,
And mateless wives grow timid at the Ocean's fearful roar,
'Tis then a gloom comes o'er me, and with many a plaintive sob
I long for quaint Nantucket and for Benny Cleveland's job.

In days of old brave knights were wont to guard the ladies fair
Or rescue lovely maidens from the robber baron's lair;
But on no such quest chivalric was our Benny forced to roam.
He kept his knightly vigil each night at some dame's home.

His fee as Guardian Angel all Nantucketers well knew:
'Twas fifteen cents for one night or twenty-five for two.
So, trustful in his watchfulness, wives gave themselves to sleep,
To dream of absent husbands in their journeys o'er the deep.

And husbands tossed in fragile craft 'midst wild, tempestuous
   seas
Gave little fear, for loving hearts who lived at home at ease,

While, confident as Faith itself, they knew they none could rob
Their Lares and Penates when Ben was on the job.

To his fathers Ben's been gathered these many, many years,
But no memory is more cherished in the mind of Island dears,
And, while gossiping at sewing-bees, they oft love to recall
The halcyon days when Benny was protector of them all.

Now, having met the 'Tucket girls, 'tis very clear to me
That Benny was a wise old owl, and excessive was his fee;
For, free of charge, on stormy nights, you bet that up I'd bob
To try to displace Benny from his most alluring job.

So, when portents are abroad at night and tempests lash the
   shore,
And mateless wives grow timid at the Ocean's fearful roar,
I know you cannot blame me if, with many a wistful sob,
I long for quaint Nantucket and for Benny Cleveland's job.

                                        JOSEPH A. CAMPBELL
August 1910

The annual Town Meeting is the high point of the political
year, for this is the opportunity for every citizen of the Town to
comment on any aspect of the Town government, including any
public official, and many avail themselves of the chance. Every
Town Meeting has its characters, usually a few hardy perennials
who lie dormant all year but awaken to unleash a torrent of wit
or wisdom at the meeting, gaining self-satisfaction though losing
listeners. Some profess interest in only one Town issue each year;
others claim expertise upon the entire panorama of government.
Each orator has his or her own style, supporters, and critics, and
each provokes a volley of cheers or groans from the audience.
The modern Town Meetings are models of decorum in comparison with those of past decades when the sheriff was called upon
to read the Riot Act, and when "A spittoon having been hurled at
the Moderator, the Meeting was declared Adjourned."
   At the meeting, one may always depend upon some layman
rising in rebuttal to a lawyer's argument or a Town Counsel ruling and starting his remarks with, "I'm not a lawyer, but . . . ," a
phrase which is certain to introduce a lengthy legal opinion. One

such solid citizen always opposed any sale of Town real estate by solemnly assuring the townsfolk that he had seen it plainly written in a law book in the court house that a town could never sell its land. When questioned about the source of this curbstone opinion, he repeated that he had read it in a law book some time ago, but when he tried to find it the day before the Town Meeting, the book was missing! Plainly implying that anyone capable of stealing a law book would not hesitate to steal the Town's land, he always managed to kill the sale.

The Nantucket representative always had an unusual variety of requests to present for legislative action, but since the Island's demands were few, he could usually obtain what was needed.[1] One year the islanders wanted a bicycle path to 'Sconset; another year, permission to buy up the remaining sheep commons on the Island. A curious legislative act resulted when the Town police force went on Civil Service, only to discover that one of its favorite policemen, George Rezendes, who stood five feet five inches tall, was one inch too short for Civil Service requirements. The "Short Cop Bill" waived the minimum height requirement for Nantucket and it provoked a spirited debate in the Senate, but finally passed when Senator Kevin B. Harrington, who stood six feet nine inches, quoted Lincoln to the effect that, "A man's legs should be just long enough to reach the ground."

We were fortunate to be present in the House of Representatives on a memorable occasion when Massachusetts proudly honored its pre-eminent native son shortly before his inauguration as President of the United States. In January of 1961, John F. Kennedy addressed the General Court, delivering his famous "City Upon a Hill" speech. It was a thrilling and historic event as the young President-elect spoke in the ancient chamber of the House and his eloquence matched the occasion. It was a day

[1] In 1956, Robert F. Mooney, while a student at Harvard Law School, received special permission from Dean Erwin Griswold to serve as Nantucket's State Representative. Subsequently, he obtained the nomination of both parties and thus became the only Democrat-Republican in the State House. André R. Sigourney served in the legislature representing the small peninsula town of Nahant, which juts into Boston Harbor, connected to the mainland by a long causeway. Nahant is geographically the smallest town in Massachusetts and contained approximately the same population as Nantucket at that time. Our similar political backgrounds led to remarkably similar experiences during our terms in the House from 1957 through 1970.

bright with promise of a great future for him and for the country. We did not realize it was his farewell to Massachusetts.

The Nantucket representative never forgot one memorable moment which concerned a famous object of Massachusetts pride, the striking statue of Civil War General Joseph Hooker astride his prancing war-horse which stands outside the front entrance of the State House. Nantucket was the banner town in the Commonwealth during the Civil War; it sent 339 men into the Union forces, many of them serving under General Hooker at Chancellorsville. To honor the dashing commander of the Army of the Potomac, the sculptor faithfully portrayed him and his horse in faithful detail. As the statue stands on a pedestal fifteen feet in the air, each detail of the glorious, life-size, virile horse is vividly apparent to everyone entering the State House.

During one legislative session which lasted into the evening, the House was debating the merits of a proposed law for dealing with sex offenders. One of the popular proposals of the time called for the mandatory castration of sex offenders, and in the prevailing mood of Massachusetts politics, such drastic punishment seemed likely to become law. A few lawyers in the House mentioned the constitutional prohibition against "cruel and unusual punishment," but it soon became evident that the legislators and spectators were not interested in legal trivia that evening; they wanted blood.

As the bill neared its final noisy approval in the House, one legislator, noted for his wisdom and shrewd in his appraisal of the legislative atmosphere, rose to be recognized. "Mr. Speaker," he said, "I would like to offer a simple amendment to this bill—just one sentence. 'Provided, however, this law shall not apply to legislators, past or present, nor to General Hooker's horse.'" That was the end of the bill—and an appropriate end of the subject.

The legislative history of Nantucket was a continuously fascinating saga, but the most important legislation in the history of the modern Island was the culmination of a twelve-year struggle over the vital issue of the Steamship Authority. In 1948 the legislature established a public corporation, the imaginatively named New Bedford, Woods Hole, Martha's Vineyard and Nantucket Steamship Authority, to take over the steamship service to the Island which had previously been owned by the rapidly failing New Haven Railroad. For many years the Authority was the center of political controversy with the island communities usually fighting against the interest of the mainland terminal in New Bedford, which had an economic interest in preserving its contacts with the islands. Each year the Authority amassed an increasing deficit, which was assessed on the ports served in varying proportions. After several lawsuits went to the Supreme Judicial Court, it was decided that New Bedford was entitled to daily, year-round service. The islands (probably for the first time in history) united to propose a radical new solution to the legislature.

In 1960, Nantucket and Martha's Vineyard representatives sponsored a bill to reorganize the Steamship Authority by dropping New Bedford overboard, leaving the two islands (with the cooperation of Woods Hole) to pay their own bills and control their own economic destiny. So convinced were the islanders of their position that they spurned the possibility of a state subsidy and the financial benefits of the New Bedford connection; after all, the boat line existed only to serve the islands, and the one mainland port of Woods Hole should be sufficient.

This major reorganization of the Steamship Authority was proposed in the House as the Sylvia-Mooney Bill, and was carried in the Senate by the veteran Senator Edwin C. Stone. It received great editorial support from Editor Henry Beetle Hough of the *Vineyard Gazette* and Joseph Indio of the *Nantucket Town Crier*. A well-organized island campaign secured the support of island visitors and summer residents all over the state, who convinced their own legislators to support the islands' cause. The New Bedford-based labor unions called a strike at the start of the summer season of 1960, which paralyzed service for six weeks, but served only to convince the public of the islands' dependence on the steamship line. The bill sailed through the House by a wide margin.

The New Bedford forces then concentrated their efforts on the forty-member Massachusetts Senate, where the pressure was the greatest. New Bedford had on its side the voting weight of a large urban population, a solid labor organization, and the power of the only daily newspaper in southeastern Massachusetts, the

New Bedford *Standard Times*. The powerful leader of the State Senate, John E. Powers, a Democratic dynamo who seldom lost a crucial vote, had always supported New Bedford in the past.

At this crucial point, a special election in New Bedford resulted, sending a Republican to the Senate. The Democrats were furious at the loss of a "safe" seat, and Senate President Powers decided he'd had enough of this steamship business. When the bill hit the Senate, Republican Senator Stone argued eloquently for the cause of the islands, knowing all the time that a party-line vote would kill it. Then President Powers left the chair, took the floor, and roared his defiance of the city which had the effrontery to claim Democratic votes after electing a Republican senator. The Democrats got the message, and the bill passed the Senate by a healthy margin.

The fate of the Steamship Authority then landed in the lap of Democratic Governor Foster Furcolo, who had previously been considered allied to the heavy voting power of the City of New Bedford (though, ironically, in September 1960, Governor Furcolo was defeated in a Democratic primary election for U. S. Senator). When the Steamship Bill landed on his desk, Governor Furcolo bided his time, and twice asked for extensions of the deadline for his signature. He referred the bill to the Democratic Attorney General, Edward J. McCormack, who ruled in favor of its constitutionality.

Late in October 1960, Governor Furcolo signed into law the Steamship Authority Reorganization Bill. The news was greeted with jubilation by the islanders, who felt pride and vindication in their first legislative victory after a twelve-year struggle to win control of their steamship line. The islanders were especially grateful for the help and support they received from legislators from all over the state who had responded to their pleas for independence, and from the leading political figures who had risen to aid their cause. Within a few years, the Steamship Authority delivered increasingly efficient service to the islands and became the first profitable public transport company in the state. By 1978 it was the only public transportation entity in the country able to operate without a public subsidy.

Nantucket's last chapter in the saga of state politics occurred in the hectic summer of 1977, when a curious combination of history and circumstances united to ring down the curtain on Nantucket's colorful role in the State Legislature. It all began with the U. S. Supreme Court decision in *Baker* v. *Carr* (1962), which required state election districts to be apportioned to approximate the ideal rule of "one man, one vote." Both Nantucket and Martha's Vineyard had been entitled to one representative each in the State Legislature under a Massachusetts constitutional provision which allowed each county at least one representative, although the islands' population was far less than that of any other representative district in the state. This arrangement survived a number of court challenges over the years, with the court recognizing the unique needs of the island communities, but the Supreme Court's handwriting was on the wall.

The next assault came from the forces of reform and modernization, when a strong movement developed to reduce the membership of the Massachusetts House of Representatives from 240 to 160. The reformers were led by the League of Women Voters, the *Boston Globe,* and many other potent political forces who argued that a House of 240 was unnecessary, inefficient, and unwieldy. The public seized upon the idea, convinced that it would modernize state government and eliminate many of the perceived abuses of the legislative process. The politicians in the legislature fought it mightily, but their constituents voted overwhelmingly to cut the House down to 160 members in the election of 1974, and, in a classic example of electoral irresponsibility, both Martha's Vineyard and Nantucket voted for the change. Later voters complained that the referendum on the ballot was long and confusing, and that many islanders never realized how it would effect their representatives, but the votes were counted and the bell had tolled on the islands.

In 1976 the islands elected their last representatives to the State House, Terry McCarthy from Martha's Vineyard and J. Sydney Conway from Nantucket. They faced the forlorn task of fighting to preserve the islands' representation in the legislature, and the legislature had the unwelcome responsibility of producing a redistricting bill which would conform to the constitutional mandate, creating legislative districts of 30,000 voters each and retiring 80 of their colleagues. Both islands were put into a district with half of Cape Cod. The arrangement meant that no islander would ever again represent the area, and effectively removed the Island voters from any direct representation in the legislature.

The Island erupted in a storm of outrage and protest. The movement which gained most notoriety was directed toward Secession, with the islands leaving Massachusetts for more hospitable states which offered them refuge and representation. This would indeed have been a lawyer's dream, and the thought was tempting to the legal mind. Such a move would require an affirmative vote of two state legislatures, the signatures of two Governors, and an Act of Congress, and the legal complications of moving a thriving community from one state to another would keep the Island lawyers in business for generations. Perhaps we would have our own courts, our own laws, our own bar exams! The two islands would be in a position to strike their own bargain with any state that wanted them, and pictures of tax exemptions and free-port status danced through our minds. Maybe we would opt for independence, join the United Nations, and apply for foreign aid. The movement produced a flood of publicity. Islanders raised their own flags and issued passports to travelers from the mainland, while newspapers around the world saluted their call for independence. It seemed that the Golden Age of Nantucket might return, with the islanders dealing with England and France as equals as they had done during the whaling heyday of the nineteenth century. Alas, it was not to be. The redistricting bill sailed through the legislature and was quickly signed into law by Governor Michael Dukakis. After the state election of 1978, Nantucket and Martha's Vineyard would no longer have seats in the State House.

Thus ended a long and glorious tradition of islanders in the legislature. The Town of Nantucket, which produced Congressmen, State Senators, and many fine legislators, which once had three representatives of its own, which sent forth the venerable Micajah Coffin spouting Latin to the Governor, would never again have its own voice in the General Court of Massachusetts. Only time will tell if the new legislature is more efficient or economical. Many islanders believe that the tide of reform has swept away the personal contact the island communities had with the state government, and by removing government further from the people, has buried a precious part of their heritage in the shifting sands of state politics.

Appendix

*General Laws, made at the firſt Generall Court,
holden at* EDGARTOWNE, *upon* MARTHA'S
VINEYARD, *the 18th of June, 1672.*

[Deeds i, 78, Secretary's Office.]

Ordered by this Court, That the Gen^all Court ſhall Annually beginn, either upon the firſt Tueſday in June, or *upon* the firſt convenient Opportunity in reſpect of Weather.

Ordered, That the Preſident ſhall be allowed for each Dayes Loſſe in attending this Court ſix Shillings per day; and each Magiſtrate four Shillings: which Charge ſhall be allowed and paid out of the Treaſury, and at the Quarter Court of each Iſland, the Preſident ſhall bee allowed three Shillings per day, and each Affiſtant two Shillings and ſix pence per day.

Ordered, That each Iſland ſhall hold and keep foure Courts a Yeare at *Martha's Vineyard,* the laſt Tueſday of March, the laſt Tueſday of June, the laſt Tueſday of September, and the laſt Tueſday in December: And at *Nantuckett* the laſt Tueſday in Ffebruary, the laſt Tueſday in June, the laſt Tueſday in September, and the laſt Tueſday in December.

Ordered by this Court, That if any Perſon ſhall finde himſelfe Aggrieved in any Sentence given by the Quarter Court in either Iſland, the Caſe being above five Pounds, hee ſhall have Liberty to appeale to the next Gen^all Court, which if it ſhall happen to bee held at the ſame Iſland, where Judgment was before given, the Perſon appealing ſhall if hee ſee Cauſe have ſix Jurors from the other Ifland, and the Party caft fhall in fuch Cafe pay to fuch Jurors two Shillings fix pence per day, for every Day fuch Jurors loofe in attending yᵉ Court by their Meanes. Or if hee fee not Caufe to bee at that Charge, he may enter his Appeale unto the next Generall Court to bee holden at the other Ifland, where he fhall have Liberty of a Jury for the Tryall of his Caufe.

Always provided, that the Aggrieved Perfon enter his Appeale during the Sitting of yᵉ Court hee appealeth from, and in fuch Appeale hee fhall give in Bond for the Profecution of his Appeale to effect, when hee fhall bring noe other Evidence nor Plea, but the fame which was given in, unto the Court appealed from.

It's Ordered, That any Perfon fhall have Liberty at Quarter Courts to review his Caufe, provided hee hath fome new Matter or Evidence, wᶜʰ Review fhall bee at the next Quarter Court, unleffe the Court fhall fee Caufe to give him a longer Time. And if it appeare to the Court where fuch Review is heard, that it is only to keep his Adverfary from his Right, hee fhall pay double Damages.

Ordered, That noe Man's Perfon fhall be Arrefted or Imprifoned for Debt or Ffine, if any competent Meanes of Satisfaction can bee found otherwife from his Eftate, which fhall bee made and apprized as neare as may bee to what is contracted, for in Cafes of Contract, by Perfons appointed thereunto by the Court: But if no fuch Eftate can be found, then his Perfon may be Arrefted and Imprifoned, where hee fhall bee kept upon his own, not upon the Plaintiffs Charges, until Satisfaction be made, unleffe the Court fhall fee Caufe to the Contrary. Provided nevertheleffe, That no Mans Perfon fhall bee kept in Prifon for Debt, unleffe there be an Appearance of fome Eftate which hee will not produce; In which Cafe the Court may adminifter an Oath to the Perfon indebted, and likewife to any Perfon fufpected to have fuch Eftate in his Keeping: And in fuch Cafe his Perfon fhall bee fold for Satisfaction, but neither out of the Country, nor to any other but the Englifh Nation, neither fhall bee Tranfported out of the Country, unleffe by his own Confent.

Ordered, That any Plaintiff may take out a Summons or Attachment againft any Defendant: Provided that no Attachment in any Civill Action fhall be Granted to a Fforeigner againft any fettled Inhabitant unleffe hee give fufficient Security, and Caution to Profecute his Action, and to Anfwer the Defendant fuch Cofts and Charges as the Court fhall award him.

Ordered, That in all Attachm^{ts} of Goods and Chattells, or of Lands and Hereditaments, Legall Notice fhall bee given to the Party, or left in Writing at his Houfe or Place of ufuall Abode; otherwife the Suite fhall not proceed. But if hee bee out of Jurifdiction, the Cafe fhall then proceed to Tryall, but Judgment fhall not enter until the next Court: And if the Defendant doe not then appeare, Judgment fhall bee entered, but Execution fhall not be Granted before the Plaintiff hath given in fufficient Security to bee refponfible to the Defendant, if hee fhall reverfe the Judgment within one Yeare, or fuch farther Time as the Court fhall limit.

Ordered, That all Warrants, Summons, or Attachm^{ts} fhall be ferved fix Days before the Court.

Ordered, That all Perfons fummoned by Sub-Pœna to give Teftimony in any Caufe fhall give in their Evidence in Writing; And if the Evidence bee in relation to any Cafe upon the Ifland where fuch Perfon dwelleth, hee fhall then perfonally attend the Court to give in his Evidence, but if hee dwell upon any other Ifland within this Jurifdiction, hee may deliver his Evidence before any one Magiftrate, unleffe hee fhall bee required by the Perfon caufing him to bee Sup-Penad to appeare Viva Voce: And in fuch Cafe the Perfon foe requiring fhall be at the whole Charge, which fhall bee two fhillings fix pence per Day. And all others giving Evidence fhall have allowed them two fhillings per Day, which fhall bee paid by the Perfon laft.

Ordered, That all Evidence receiv'd in Court fhall bee Recorded, and ye ffees for Recording fhall bee fix pence per Teftimony.

Ordered, That all Men dyeing Inteftate, their Widdowes fhall have one third Part of all Land and ffree-hold, with all Priveledges and Appurtenances thereunto belonging during their Naturall Lives, which did anywife belong to their Hufbands; which at their Death fhall Returne to ye Right Heyres: And one third Part of all their moveable Eftate forever.

Ordered, That whofoever fhall openly or willingly defame any Court of Juftice, or the Sentences or Proceedings of the fame, or any of the Magiftrates or other Judges of any Court in refpect of any Act or Sentence therein paffed, and being legally Con-

victed thereof fhall bee Punifhed by Whipping, Ffine, Imprifon-
ment, Disfranchifement, as the quality and meafure of the
Offence fhall deferve.

Ordered, That if any Perfon fhall afk Councell or Advice of
any Magiftrate in any Cafe wherein hee fhall or may bee P^{lt}, before fuch Magiftrate hee fhall bee difenabled to Profecute any
fuch Action, that hee hath foe Advifed about at the next Court
where his Caufe fhall come to Tryall: Being pleaded by way of
Barr, either by the Defend^t or any on his Behalfe; in which Cafe
the Plaintiff fhall pay full Coft to the Defendant. And if the
Defend^t fhall afk Councell as aforefaid, hee fhall pay ten Shillings
to the Plaintiffe.

Ordered, That if any Perfon fhall bee Accufed by any, either
Indian or any other Perfon whatfoever, to have fold or furnifhed
any Indyan or Indyans with Wine, Liquor, or any Strong Drink,
Beer only excepted, hee fhall either purge himfelfe by Oath,
That hee hath neither fold, given, lent, nor anywayes directly or
indirectly furnifhed fuch Indian or Indyans with any Quantity or
Quantityes, nor any Quantity under fuch Quantity or Quantityes
as hee is Accufed for: Or if hee fhall not foe purge himfelfe hee
fhall pay for fuch Offence after the Rate of five Shillings per
Pinte, for every Quantity foe fold or difpofed of. Always provided, That any who have been known to make Scruple in Con-
fcience of fwearing according to the Ufuall Cuftome, may purge
himfelfe by Subfcription.

Ordered, That if any Perfon bee found drunken, foe as to
bee difenabled either in Speech or Gefture, fhall pay ten Shillings.

Ordered, That noe Perfon fhall fell any Liquor, Wine, Beer,
or other Strong Drink by Retayle, that is, Liquor, Wine, Spirits,
or the like, under one Gallon; nor Beere, Syder, or the like under
the Barrell or Quarter Cafk, unleffe hee have Licence from the
Quarter Court, under Penalty of ye Forfeiture of five Pounds for
fuch Offence. And it fhall not be lawfull for any Inhabitant to
tarry in any fuch Licenfed Houfe above halfe an Houre at one
Time upon Penalty of paying five Shillings, unleffe hee can render fome fufficient Reafon to the Satisfaction of fuch Magiftrate,
or Court where he anfwereth his Default.

Ordered, That any Quarter Court fhall have Power to Grant

Licenfe unto fuch as they fhall think fitt to keep a Houfe of Publick Entertainment to fell Liquor, Wine, Beer, or any like Strong Drink by Retaile wth fuch Limitations and Cuftoms as to fuch Court fhall feem meet.

Ordered, That the Conftable in each Towne fhall have one Man added to him, and they two fhall bee a Grand Jury for Prefentments, who fhall faithfully prefent to the Court whatfoever they know to bee a Breach of Law: and all fuch Criminall Matters they apprehend prefentable.

Ordered, That all Weights and Meafures fhall bee of the fame Quantityes that the Weighs and Meafures of Winchefter in England are; three ffoot to the Yard, twelve Inches to the Foot, eight Gallons to the Bufhell, and fixteen Ounces to the Pound, and foe proportionably for greater or leffer Weights and Meafures. And if any Perfon fhall prefume to ufe any other Weights or Meafures, but fuch as fhall bee fealed, hee fhall pay for fuch Offence ten fhillings.

Ordered, That noe Perfon whatfoever, not Inhabiting within this Jurifdiction fhall directly or indirectly either by himfelfe or ffactour, or any from, or under him trade or traffique wth any Indyan or Indians anywhere, either in Harbour, Creek, Cove, or on Shore within this Jurifdiction without Leave or Liberty, firft had and obtained from the Generall Court, upon Penalty of paying for foe trading the Value of twenty Shillings, the full Summe of fourty Pounds. And it is hereby Ordered, That the Water Bailiffe fhall have full Power and Authority to ftopp any Veffell, Barque, Ketch, or any other like Veffell, according to Warrant, which hee fhall to that End receive from fome Magiftrate: And if the Mafter or Merchant of any fufpected Veffell having fuch Trade on Board as ufually is the Produce of thefe Places, cannot make appeare where they had fuch Trade, hee or they fhall bee accounted guilty of the Breach of this Law.

Ordered by the Court, That each Ifland fhall choofe a Treafurer, who fhall receive and difburfe according to Order from the Court; who fhall bee fatisfied for fuch Trouble by twelve Pence in the Pound, and fhall be freed from Towne and Countrey Rates.

Ordered, That the Secretary fhall have allowed him three Pounds per Annum, befides his other ffees.

Ordered, That each Juror fhall be allowed fix Pence per Action for every Action that fhall be entered; and every Plaintiff fhall pay for entering his Action, five Shillings, which fhall goe into the Publique Treafury. And all Charge of Court fhall bee paid in Money, Corne or ffeathers.

Ordered, That every Conftable fhall have for his Serving of a Warrant or Summons for an Attachment twelve Pence, for an Execution two Pence; And if it bee in the Liberty of any Conftable in Executions to add all neceffary Charges thereto. And if any Perfon fhall Refufe to Affift a Conftable in the Execution of his Office upon his Command, he fhall Forfeit fourty Shillings. And it is Ordered, That noe Man by an Execution upon Judgment fhall be deprived of anything which moft nearly concerns his Livelyhood, as Working Cattle, Working Tools, Bedd, or Bedding, Provifion, neceffary Houfehold Stuffe, and the like, where any other Satisfaction can be found.

Ordered, That if any Perfon fhall ftrike a Conftable in the Execution of his Office, hee fhall pay foure Pounds or more, as the Circumftances of the Cafe fhall appeare: which Payment fhall be as a ffine to y[e] Countrey, which notwithftanding fhall not abridge fuch Conftable of Action againft fuch Perfon. And any one who fhall affront another in y[e] Prefence of the Court, hee fhall be feverely punifhed, or fined according to the Meritt and Nature of the Offence, by the Court where fuch Offence is done.

All Wills fhall be proved at the next Quarter Court after the Partyes Deceafe.

Hee that fhall fweare or curfe, not being legally called thereunto, fhall pay ten Shillings.

Ordered, That any Indyan fhall have Liberty in any Cafe to appeale from fuch Courts as they fhall hold amongft themfelves to the Quarter Court, and from any Quarter Court to the Generall Court, according to Law.

Ordered, That in all Actional and Criminall Matters and Cafes which fall not under the Head of fome of thefe Laws already made, fhall be Tryed, and Judgment or Sentence given according to the Laws of England.

This is a True Copie given by mee this 28th of June, 1672.

MATTHEW MAYHEW, *Secr.*

Recorded Novem: the 9th, 1674.